THE TAILOR'S DAUGHTER

1st Edition

Published in 2014 by
Woodfield Publishing Ltd
Bognor Regis PO21 5EL England
www.woodfieldpublishing.co.uk

Copyright © 2014 Joan Blackburn

All rights reserved

This publication is protected by international law.
No part of its contents may be copied, reproduced or
transmitted in any form or by any means, electronic
or mechanical, or be stored in any information
storage & retrieval system, without prior permission
in writing from Woodfield Publishing Ltd

The right of Joan Blackburn to be identified as
author of this work has been asserted in accordance
with the Copyright, Designs and Patents Act 1988

ISBN 1-84683-162-8

Printed and bound in England

Typesetting & page design: Nicolai Pastorius
Cover design: Klaus Berger

The Tailor's Daughter

*Adventures of Charlotte Adshead
1858-1929*

JOAN BLACKBURN

Joan Blackburn

Woodfield

Woodfield Publishing Ltd
Bognor Regis ~ West Sussex ~ England ~ PO21 5EL
tel 01243 821234 ~ **e/m** info@woodfieldpublishing.co.uk

Interesting and informative books on a variety of subjects

For full details of all our published titles, visit our website at
www.woodfieldpublishing.co.uk

for
Jacob, Alice, Harvey and Keira

~ CONTENTS ~

	Introduction	*ii*
1.	(Autumn 1883) Introducing the Adsheads	1
2.	The Seed Grows	12
3.	Plans for an Adventure	23
4.	The Adventure Begins	36
5.	Introducing the Gosleys	51
6.	Happiness and Tragedy	63
7.	A Change in Circumstances	84
8.	The Journey Home	96
9.	A stay in London	111
10.	New Horizons	122
11.	The Lodging House	137
12.	(1899) Big Changes	145
13.	In Mother's footsteps	163
14.	(1913) "The War to end all Wars"	187
15.	A New Dawn	208
	About the Author	*222*

Introduction

It is 1883 and twenty-five year old Charlotte Adshead felt like life was passing her by. Born in Clapham, London, she had spent all her life since the age of fourteen working in the service of the gentry and had yet to be swept off her feet by a handsome beau. Her father, a tailor, had taught her to sew and her mother had made sure she could cook. "After all" he had said, "if you can cook and sew you will never be hungry". But she wanted more out of life and seized her opportunity when she saw an advert in the newspaper for people to settle in New Zealand. After the initial shock to her parents she embarked, on her own, on what would turn out to be a defining moment in her life and that of all her descendents to follow. They say a 'split second decision in the life of one generation can change the whole future for the next'. Never was this more so when Charlotte met the cocky sailor, Frederick Gosley.

1. (Autumn 1883) Introducing the Adsheads

The sky was a leaden grey and there were a few spots of rain as Charlotte Adshead hurried from the train station at Cambridge and strode quickly along the road towards the mansion owned by her employer. The journey from London had been uncomfortable in the new fangled steam train but it was far superior than having to travel by horse and cart from her home in Clapham.

She lifted her skirts above her ankles and dodged the puddles from the last deluge. It had been a miserable autumn and it seemed a long time to wait until the summer. Moreover, she was starting to get fed up with her life as a Parlour Maid in the home of a retired Admiral and his wife.

"Don't be silly Charlotte" she chided herself "the family are very good to you – stop being an ungrateful wretch."

They were good to her too. She had just enjoyed two full days at home which was one more than the usual one day a month that most servants got. Her mind drifted back to a few hours before when she had been amid the hustle and bustle of her large family.....

❖ ❖ ❖

Charlotte's father was a skilled tailor and a true cockney having been born within the sound of Bow Bells back in 1832, even before Princess Victoria succeeded her Uncle William the Fourth to the throne. Times had moved on and it was 1883 now and hard to believe that we were hurtling towards 1884. She smiled to herself when she thought of her little brother Thomas growing up in this ever changing world. Bless him, he was just ten and suffered no less than eight sisters. The poor boy did not know where he was for skirts!

She was the second of the Adshead girls. Her older sister, Julia had been married for a few years now and both twenty-two year old Ellen and twenty-one year old Minnie were also married. Amy who was sixteen was in service, just as she was, but the other girls Fanny who was fourteen, Alice aged twelve and Annie five and young Thomas were all still at home so even though three had gone, it was still cramped despite the house at 10 Crichton Street, Clapham being quite large with three good sized bedrooms and a box room which her young brother occupied. At least there he could shut himself away and get a bit of peace from the mountains of pantaloons, stays and bodices.

It had been a lovely two days though. Father was preoccupied with his new sewing machine which allowed the girls to have fun and go out and about around London without him being too cross when they came in all untidy after running around the park. He had been a tailor all his life and that had been learned at the knee of his late father Jonathan who was also in the same business.

"After all my boy" Jonathan had said to him, "there are two things that people will always need, food and clothes – if you can't earn a living at one or the other then there is something wrong with you."

Thomas had passed this philosophy on to his brood of children.

His wife was also called Charlotte and she was just happy to have her children – or most of them – altogether for a change, despite the extra work and the chaos. She had already made up her mind that she was never ever going to have them all together at any one time again. It was getting too much. They were all gradually going their separate ways though. It was inevitable.

Thomas had been a good husband to her and had provided for the family with his tailoring skills. In fact he was very much in demand as more people came into London to take advantage of the employment and the new modern way of life.

Both Thomas and Charlotte were very much of the old ways and could barely keep up with this new Victorian age, an age of steam trains and sewing machines and, in some parts of London, electric light! There were even, would you believe, trains that travelled underneath the ground, like huge moles, to take people to their places of business without having to cope with the traffic and confusion of the busy London streets! Everywhere was a melee of people and various forms of horse drawn carriages as hundreds of people flocked into the City in a bid to make their fortunes. It was getting difficult to even cross the road without stepping in front of a horse drawn bus, and now, there were even 'horseless carriages' as well!! It was just unthinkable and Thomas wondered how it was going to be possible for the one to share the same street with the other, and would the cobbled streets cave in onto the underground trains below?

Charlotte Senior was a Wiltshire lass who had come up to London with her own parents back in the eighteen thirties when she was still a baby. She had met and married Thomas, the cheeky Cockney, and never regretted one single minute. Thomas came from a very broken family of Londoners. His father Jonathan had been married four times! Four times! Charlotte couldn't believe it when she was told.

"He was just a glutton for punishment!" laughed Thomas when his wife showed her surprise at the number of wives he'd had.

Thomas's mother was Jonathan's second wife so already he had step sisters. She died while Thomas was still a baby and after that there were yet two more stepmothers and a number of step brothers and sisters, so there were siblings all over London. No wonder he was happy to settle in Clapham with his wife and his tailoring business and get away from the chaotic home.

Charlotte could not remember her grandfather Jonathan who died soon after she was born but she had heard so many tales about the cheeky cockney that she felt she did know him. Apparently he had been a lovable rogue of a man and the fact that he had been married four times gave testament to that.

All the girls had taken turns in helping their father with the tailoring and Charlotte was no exception but eventually it had been time to move on and make way for the younger ones to help out. All had to go out into the wider world eventually, unless of course they were lucky enough to find good husbands.

So far she had not done so and it was with a certain amount of regret that she had gone to the Agency to apply for a job as a Parlour Maid. At first she had been horrified when she was told that the only Parlour Maid's job available was right up in Cambridgeshire. It seemed such a long way off to one who had never set foot outside London. However, it had given her a degree of independence and a thirst for adventure which was unsettling.

❖ ❖ ❖

The threatened rain started to come down with a vengeance just as Charlotte reached the servant's entrance of the Mansion and farms owned by retired Admiral Brownlow and Lady Brownlow. She hurried down the stone steps to the big kitchen where the cook was already preparing the evening meal.

"Goodness Charlotte, look at you, you look like something the master's dog has just dragged in. Go and get changed quickly dear and be ready to come and help serve dinner."

"Yes Cook"

She removed her hat, and her hair which had been rolled up tidily around her head, started to fall down around her shoulders as she hurried to her little room to change into her uniform of black dress with white apron and white lacy cap.

"Oh gawd, I know I'm back" thought Charlotte to herself, "looks like I had better not upset Cook today."

In actual fact Charlotte quite liked the Cook. She was a homely woman called Mrs. Catchpole, but everybody just called her Cook. As far as everyone was concerned she was the most important person in the house and she was considered to be in charge of the staff.

Charlotte had a quick wash in the cold water in the jug and basin which were on her little table at the side of her bed and got herself dressed. She took a deep breath.

"Back to the grind." She grimaced.

It was a long day being a Parlour Maid and she knew she would be on the go until at least ten thirty this evening and would be up again at five thirty the following morning. Not for the first time she started to wonder if this was really the life for her.

She wanted adventure. She didn't see why it should always be the men getting all the fun. She thought of that great woman Florence Nightingale. She had managed to do what she wanted to do. Not that she wanted to be a nurse like that great lady, but just something different from being a Parlour Maid in Cambridge. Besides, she was nearly twenty-five and she still hadn't found herself a young man! There had been a few back in London who had made eyes at her, but none that she wanted to give any encouragement to. The master's valet was always asking her to walk out with him, but so far she had declined. She did not feel drawn towards him and he wasn't exactly the brightest knife in the drawer! Clearly she was too fussy, but certainly, if she did not find a husband, then she wanted something more out of life.

She rushed into the kitchen just in time to take the tray from Cook and, along with Susan, the other Parlour Maid, they carried the food into the dining room ready to serve up to the family who were already seated.

"Ah Charlotte dear, you are back!" boomed the Admiral. "We have missed you dear – did you have a nice time?"

She put the potatoes in the tureen on the table while Susan served the meat.

"Yes, thank you Sir". She bobbed a curtsey, and poured water into a glass for Lady Eleanor Brownlow. She was a timid little woman, as slight and slim as her husband was robust and fat. Charlotte wondered what he had been like as a boss in charge of a ship. Of course it was some years ago and he would have been slimmer and fitter then.

John the butler came into the room and served the wine. He had been a military man too, but in the Army and it showed. He had a back as straight as a ramrod and he ruled the kitchen with a rod of iron too. There was some discrepancy between himself and the Cook as to who was properly in charge!

Charlotte took a glance around the table at the rest of the family. There was the Admiral's two sons William and George and their wives and each had two children. Also visiting were Lady Brownlow's sister Muriel and her husband Albert. By now all were lost in their own conversations as the two girls and James stood in the background ready to attend to their every need.

Admiral Augustus Brownlow made short work of his piece of beef and engaged himself in conversation with his brother-in-law who was also a sailor, although much more recently. He was up to speed on all things new and Augustus enjoyed talking to him about his days on the sea which had included service on the ships involved in the Crimea.

"Ah those were the days my boy – the days of sail, when you could rely on the wind and a ships compass. I doubt I could cope with all this modern steam and steel."

"Its not that new" replied Albert. "The steel hull was invented thirty or more years ago as you very well know." He put his knife and fork down and supped some of his red wine.

"Things don't stand still – do you know you can get to the Antipodes in the space of two or three months now?"

"Now why would anybody want to get down to that part of the world in such a short time," laughed the Admiral, "it's only convicts that go there anyway and if I were a convict I would be quite happy to take the six months or so that it takes by sail – longer in fact."

Everyone laughed but they all knew he was out of tune with the modern way.

All Charlotte wanted was for them to finish their dinner so that she could go and get hers. The two parlour maids continued to hover in the background waiting to dish up the dessert of apple pie.

"I hope cook has saved some of that for us," whispered Susan.

Augustus Brownlow looked across at Charlotte.

"And what about you young Adshead" he guffawed, "what do you think of all this nonsense of steel ships and getting to the Antipodes in a matter of months."

Charlotte wasn't even quite sure what the antipodes meant but guessed it had something to do with Australia considering they were talking about convicts.

"Oh I am sure I don't know Sir" she said. "Living near the Thames as I do I see lots of lovely ships coming and going but mostly sailing ships."

"Oh it all sounds very romantic to go on the high seas in a sailing ship" twittered Lady Eleanor, "but come on dear, lets finish our meal and let these girls get off and have theirs."

After what seemed like an interminable time they did finish and the plates were cleared away. The ladies retired to the Drawing Room and the gentlemen stayed behind for brandy and continued their discussion about the merits of steel ships that still retained their sails so that they can be converted into clippers. It was all too technical for Eleanor.

"Thank goodness for that" gasped Charlotte as the two parlour maids sat down at the table with Cook and John Walker the Butler. Thankfully Mrs Catchpole saved them a bit of dinner which was some nice slices of beef and vegetables and, for afters, some apple pie.

"Tell you what," said Susan, "I'll lock up tonight and put the lights out and then you can have an early night.

"Oh thanks Sue, it's been a bloody long day today."

It had been a long day too. She had awoken at five o'clock that morning to the sound of horses and wooden wheels on the cobbles all struggling to get around the congested streets along with the occasional horseless carriage or motor car. Then there was a bit of time with all her sisters and young brother before undertaking the journey in the steam train followed by a very long walk and then the evenings work. Moreover she would be expected to rise at six o'clock the following morning ready to brush the master's clothes and tidy up the drawing room. Suddenly the idea of a ship off to the antipodes seemed very appealing!

Even now her day wasn't over, she still had to see the visitors off the premises and take in bedtime drinks to Lord and Lady Brownlow.

The one thing about this household though was that the staff did muck in together and cook had already done most of the washing up. She liked Mrs. Catchpole – she was a good woman who made the life of a parlour maid much easier. Not all cooks for the gentry were like that.

Even so, by the time Charlotte said goodnight to Susan it was ten o'clock and all she wanted was her bed.

"Why can't I find a husband" she said to herself as she walked down the corridor to the little room that she shared with Susan, "I'm too fussy, that's my trouble."

She looked at her reflection in the mirror. What she saw before her wasn't bad – people always said she was very pretty, and her crowning glory was her long dark hair which she usually wore rolled up all around her head. The pulled the pins out and it cascaded around her shoulders. Admittedly she was slightly plumper than she would have liked to have been, most people would have called her a 'comely wench' but her older sister Julia was plumper than her and she had managed to find herself a beau.

She got undressed and put her dressing gown on and then hurried along to the servant's lavatory before having a quick wash and falling into bed. She was asleep in an instant and didn't even hear Susan creeping into the room and settling down for the night almost an hour later.

She slept soundly but was awake before the cockerel and quickly flew out of bed at the same time as Susan.

"Beat you to the lavatory" laughed Susan as she rushed for the door.

"Oh no, I'll beat you!" giggled Charlotte, "you haven't even got your dressing gown on yet."

The two girls jostled each other about as they rushed to get ready. Charlotte put on her printed morning dress and white apron and cap and had a last look at herself in the mirror before rushing out and joining the rest of the staff in the kitchen. There would be just time to have some breakfast before getting on with the first of the days duties which was cleaning and tidying the dining room.

She helped herself to a ladle full of porridge from the big saucepan on the kitchen range and sat down at the wooden table. All the talk was of the latest immigrants to Australia and New Zealand.

"Why would anybody want to go all that way?" said Cook. "It's thousands and thousands of miles."

"But getting easier all the time" said John, "and you can get an assisted passage so it is not too much money."

"How much?" said Susan

"Fifteen pounds" I think, said John.

"What! Fifteen pounds" Cook threw her apron over her face in a gesture of shock and horror. "Fifteen pounds!" "That's a years wages for some people."

"It's a years wages for me!" said Charlotte and Susan both at the same time.

The talk was interrupted as Mrs. Catchpole looked at the clock on the wall and realised that the day had begun for the rest of the household too.

"Right come on you girls" she said "time for talking is over, let's get on and get busy."

"And you lot too" added John as he ushered George the valet and Sam the groom on their way.

The days work had started in the Brownlow household but a seed had been planted in Charlotte's mind that would germinate in the fullness of time.

❖ ❖ ❖

2. The Seed Grows

"Fancy living in a posh place like this." said Susan as the two girls busied themselves cleaning silver and polishing the woodwork in the Drawing Room. "I could get used to this given half the chance."

"I dunno" replied Charlotte, "My parents have given me quite a comfortable life really – nothing like this of course, but we have never starved and father has always kept a roof over our heads. I don't know if I could be doing with all this opulence."

In fact Augustus Brownlow had inherited the Mansion and the farm attached to it from his father before him. He had been put through Naval College and had gone to sea but he always had this to fall back on whenever his father died and his seafaring days were over.

Charlotte carefully arranged the flowers in the big bowl.

"We are what we are." She said, "I think much of life is an accident of birth."

"Well I wouldn't have minded being Lady Eleanor's accident of birth," retorted Susan. She got the logs out of the big container at the side of the fire and started to make it up ready to be lit for when her employer came down to the Drawing Room, while Charlotte got on with the general dusting and brushing of the furniture.

The conversation had focussed her mind again and she found herself thinking about her father. He had worked hard, having been taught his tailoring by his father, and he had built up a good business, so much so, that the house in Clapham was quite respectable and far superior to anything that poor Susan had ever known. Moreover, Thomas had made sure that all his daughters were skilled needlewomen whilst her mother had ensured that they all could cook. The result was that she could turn her hand to anything and she was now getting to an age where she could appreciate all they had done for her. At the same time, she wanted adventure and did not foresee her life being years of toiling for Admiral Brownlow and his wife, no matter how much she admired and liked them as employers.

The doorbell rang and she went to answer it. It would be the papers for Augustus. She opened the door and the errand boy put the crisp new Times newspaper into her hand. It would be her job to iron it so that there were no creases and leave it in the drawing room.

"Just going to iron the paper" she called to Susan, and she made her way back to the kitchens and got the iron out.

"Its just slightly warm" said Mrs Catchpole, "its been on the stove."

Charlotte felt it and it was just right. She smoothed the paper and as she pressed the creases out she couldn't help but notice the picture on the front page of the new ship that would be bound for New Zealand next year, the SS British King.

"Look at that Mrs. Catchpole" she remarked, "doesn't it look grand!"

"It does indeed," she replied, "but you still wouldn't get me on it."

It was magnificent. It was a hundred and ten feet in length and weighed over three and a half thousand tons. It looked like a combination of the future and the past with its long steel hull and 2,400 horse power engines, and yet still with sail. Almost as if the engines were not quite trusted yet.

The Tailor's Daughter ~ 13

"It would be a real adventure going to New Zealand wouldn't it?" whispered Charlotte to herself, but Cook heard her.

"You wouldn't think of going on it would you?" she cried quite aghast. "it's thousands of miles away – it would be like going to another world."

"The only thing I wouldn't like is leaving my parents and family," she answered.

"Oh and not me!" laughed Mrs. Catchpole.

"Well and you of course," she thought for a minute, "but anyway I don't think it's possible. I haven't got £15 for a start – I've got some money saved up but not £15."

"Oh well, that's all right then, Mrs. Catchpole gently scoffed, "now come on and get on with what you are supposed to be doing. Take that to the Drawing room and come back here as I have a job for you young lady."

Charlotte put the iron away and hurried off to put the paper on the desk ready for the Brownlow's. Susan was still polishing the silver so she was quite glad to have something different to do no matter what it was.

"I want you to keep an eye on the ham" said Cook when she went back down to the kitchen. "I've got to go to the village for some bits of shopping for the larder and it isn't quite cooked yet – I need you to keep an eye on it and take it off the stove when it's done." She paused for a minute. "You know how to test it don't you?"

She was a bit miffed that Mrs. Catchpole could even ask such a question.

"Yes, of course, I put the skewer in and make sure it comes out clean."

"That's right, and you can still carry on with your duties, just come in and check it once in a while." She took off her apron and put on her hat and coat. "It should only need another half hour." With that she was gone.

By now Susan had gone upstairs to help the Lady's Maid in the bedrooms, Augustus went to look around the farm and Lady Eleanor retired to the Drawing Room. It was also John the Butler's day off so for a while the kitchen would be empty. Charlotte checked the ham simmering away in the big pot on the stove. It still wasn't quite done through. She decided to leave it for a while. Cook clearly wanted it to cool ready to slice for this evening's meal, probably with some potatoes and vegetables. Just then the doorbell rang and she was the only person around to answer it.

It was Lady Eleanor's sister Muriel. Charlotte helped her with her hat and coat and all the while she was chattering.

"Oh goodness me Adshead, it's cold outside. It just seems to get colder every year to me, don't you think so?"

"Yes Madam" said Charlotte. It seemed as though Muriel did not want to go – she just wanted to get warm and natter. All the while she was thinking about the ham and hoping that it would be all right.

It certainly was cold and Sam Bridges, the groom, decided to come into the kitchen for a warm. He made straight for the kitchen range and put more logs in the fire.

"That's what we need" he grunted, "a bit of warmth". He was sweetly oblivious to the large pot on the top of the stove bubbling away with the ham inside. He sat in a nearby chair and all but dozed off to sleep with the effects of the sudden heat. That is until Susan, having finished her duties for the morning, came into the kitchen, just in time to see the ham boiling over and the water sizzling and evaporating before her eyes. She grabbed a cloth and pulled the huge pot to one side.

"You stupid thing," she cried, "What have you done? The ham has boiled dry, quick, run and fetch Charlotte."

"He was just in time to see her finally extricating herself from Muriel and coming back towards the kitchen."

"I think the ham is burnt," whispered Sam so that Muriel didn't hear. "Susan says for you to come quickly."

"Oh my God!" cried Charlotte."That's all I need."

"It's boiled over and I can't get it out of the bloody pot," said Susan. "What shall we do?"

Charlotte took the pot and gently tried to scrape the ham from where it had stuck to the bottom. "Couldn't you have seen there was something on the stove?" she snarled at Sam.

"I'm so sorry."

"Go on, you had better make yourself scarce before Cook gets back" muttered Susan. Sam put on his hat and coat and wrapped a scarf around his neck and quickly took her advice.

By now Charlotte had prized the ham from the bottom of the pot and put it on a plate on the kitchen table, but a great gaping hole had appeared where she had pulled it and some of it was left stuck to the pot.

"The first time Cook gives me something to do and then this happens," she uttered. Then she suddenly remembered something her mother had taught her.

"I know Susan" she cried, "get me some of the baked breadcrumbs." Mrs. Catchpole always kept breadcrumbs that had been baked in the oven for coatings for fish and such like in the jar in the cupboard. The only other thing she needed was an egg.

"What on earth are you doing woman?" laughed Susan as she put the big jar on the table in front of Charlotte. "Oh don't tell me – I don't think I want to know. I'll start trying to clean this mess from the bottom of the pot."

"Thanks Sue."

Charlotte whisked the egg and then spread the mixture over the bottom of the ham and then sat it in the breadcrumbs. They stuck to the egg and formed a coating that covered up the hole.

"There you are" she cried triumphantly, "nobody will notice."

"Mrs Catchpole will" said Susan from the sink where she was scrubbing away at the pot.

Charlotte placed the ham, breadcrumb side down, on the serving plate. It looked for all the world as though nothing had happened.

"Bet she doesn't,"

She quickly cleared away any sign of her activity and disposed of the egg shells in the waste bin outside the kitchen door. She was just in time as Mrs Catchpole arrived back just five minutes later, and the first thing she did was look at the ham.

"That's fine Charlotte" she said "it can sit there and cool and it will be just right for dinner tonight with some potatoes and peas and a bit of salad."

Charlotte and Susan crossed their fingers behind their backs and gave each other speaking looks whilst they tried hard not to giggle. Cook never served up the main meal of the day, so with a bit of luck they would get away with it. There was just about time to have their own lunch before spending the afternoon catching up on the mending of table linen and repairs to the gentleman's clothes.

Lunch was taken around the big wooden table in the kitchen in comparative silence, and the large ham with its hidden coat of breadcrumbs seemed to leer at them from its place where it was cooling ready for the evening meal.

"I wonder if we will get away with it" giggled Charlotte as the two girls got changed into their afternoon wear of black dress and white apron.

"Well we have so far," replied Susan, "just stop looking so blooming guilty."

It was just Augustus and Lady Eleanor and Muriel for dinner today and the girls and John served the soup. All Charlotte wanted was to get it all over with, and incur the wrath of Mrs. Catchpole if she had to.

They stood with their hands behind their backs crossing and uncrossing their fingers while John sliced the ham and then they helped him to dish up the vegetables. Still nobody noticed.

"This is delicious today" said Augustus, "I like this new way of doing it. Mrs. Catchpole has excelled herself. " Charlotte and Susan tried hard not to giggle again.

"I love the crunchiness" said Eleanor, "I'll have to ask her what her secret is."

"Its breadcrumbs Madam" said Charlotte quickly, "and being cooked a little longer." The one thing she did not want was anyone confronting Cook and asking her what the new way of doing ham was!

"Well it is very nice and I will be grateful if you will pass on my compliments to Cook."

"I said we would get away with it" whispered Susan when they had their backs turned to the assembled company.

After what seemed for ever the meal was finished and Charlotte quickly grabbed hold of the plates. It would be up to her to get them into the kitchen and try and get them washed before Mrs. Catchpole detected any trace of the breadcrumbs.

"You are getting on with it aren't you dear" said Mrs. Catchpole as she looked up from the paper she was reading. "You know it is not the Parlour Maid's job to do the washing up. Leave it to the Scullery maid – she will be here in a minute."

"Oh its all right Cook!" she answered quickly, "I don't mind, oh and by the way, Lady Eleanor asked us to give you her compliments on a beautiful ham."

"Oh how nice!" Mrs. Catchpole blushed and was quite flustered. "it's not often I get compliments from her."

Charlotte smiled and finished the washing up and removed all trace of any breadcrumbs. It had been a funny old day, but she still could not put the thought of going on a ship to New Zealand out of her mind. She had ten pounds saved in the Bank. She wondered whether she could persuade her father to cough up another five pounds. She would have to find out a bit more about it first though. Indeed, she wasn't really sure how far it was. All she knew was that it was on the other side of the world. It wasn't even as though she had a prospective husband to hold her back.

The following day Charlotte had a few hours off and so she chose to do what she often did at such times. She went down to the farm to have a look at the animals and enjoy the countryside. It made such a pleasant change from the hurly burly of London. She imagined that New Zealand would be a lot like this with cattle and sheep in the green fields, and chickens running around the farmyard. Augustus left his farm hands to do the running of things but he did frequently come and oversee what was going on. It was a far cry from his days in the Navy, but it gave him something to do. He was there now as Charlotte pulled her coat around herself to shut out the winter wind.

"Hello Adshead my dear" he boomed "come to see the chickens have you."

"Yes Sir," she replied "and I'll take some eggs back for Cook."

She shivered against the cold biting November chill.

"Wrap yourself up girl," he carried on "I don't mind telling you that it is days like this that I wish I was on the high seas bound for somewhere warm."

"I expect its warm in the antipodes now Sir" said Charlotte, attempting to sound clever.

"Yes, it most certainly will be – it is high summer there."

More and more the idea of having an adventure to Australia or New Zealand appealed to her. But first she would have to confront her parents and that was not going to be easy.

The first person she told about the idea that was forming in her mind was Susan when they were having their night time drink in the servant's quarters.

"You must be mad!" cried Susan, "your family will never see you again."

"They will, it only takes a couple of months to get there in these new ships."

"What will you do when you get there?" she started to giggle, "you might end up marrying a native."

"You know I can cook," replied Charlotte, "and I can sew."

Then as an afterthought, "and who knows, I might find a rich husband."

Susan laughed, "I'm not so sure about the cooking Charlotte," she muttered, not after yesterday."

She dodged the wet floor cloth that her friend threw in her direction, but suddenly Susan felt very sad and let down.

"I'll miss you if you do go," she said, "why do you have to go all that way?"

"I don't see why it should be the men who have all the adventures" said Charlotte. "I want to see the world – I'm nearly twenty-six and this place is the most I have seen outside of

London. Anyway, it's not definite yet, I have to find out more and I have to raise the cash. Even an assisted passage is fifteen pounds."

"I certainly wouldn't want to go on my own either," went on Susan.

"Well you come then!"

"Even if I could afford it Charlotte, I would not spend the money on going all that way. Have you really any idea how far it is? It is well over three thousand miles. I can't even think about that sort of distance."

The two walked down the corridor to the servant's bathroom and met George on his way to his room. He had clearly overheard the conversation.

"What's all this?" he smiled, "talking about going off to the other side of the world are we!"

"Maybe," replied Charlotte.

"Hmm" he grunted, "not the sort of thing for a girl, not the sort of thing at all."

That did it. It was red rag to a bull. If the headstrong Charlotte had any doubts before, she certainly did not have any now. George had seen to that. It had made her even more determined to find out more about it.

Her chance came a few days later when she was ironing the newspaper for his Lordship. The cartoon on the front page sprung out at her. 'New Zealand needs Domestic Servants'. For more information apply to the High Commissioner for New Zealand in London.

The Tailor's Daughter

NEW ZEALAND
WANTS
Domestic Servants
RICH COUNTRY.
FINE CLIMATE.
GOOD WAGES.
WORK WAITING.
FARE £2.16.0.
For full particulars apply to
THE HIGH COMMISSIONER
FOR NEW ZEALAND
(EMIGRATION DEPARTMENT)
VICTORIA ST
LONDON

3.   Plans for an Adventure

People had been leaving for Australia and New Zealand since the 1850s. It was nothing new, but in the old days it had taken for ever and was often a very dangerous voyage. Now the voyage was still dangerous but it could be achieved in a couple of months. The New Zealand immigration offices were setting up all over the United Kingdom in a bid to persuade people to settle and colonise these new countries. In particular they wanted skilled labourers and domestic staff. Charlotte knew this. She wished, in a way, that she had been born some thirty years earlier for then the passage would be free, paid for by a Government who wanted to build the commonwealth. It was nearly £3 to travel steerage but she didn't really want to do that if she could help it. She was thinking about this big adventure as she bid Susan farewell and headed off home for Christmas. As usual she had two days off and Susan would have her two days when she got back. The staff was down to a bare minimum because Lord and Lady Brownlow were spending the festive season with Eleanor's sister Muriel and her husband.

There was a light flurry of snow but she was wrapped up warm in her coat and bonnet with a huge woollen scarf she had knitted around her neck. She briefly wondered if the wool she had used had come from New Zealand sheep. She envisaged that the countryside would be very similar to this countryside in Cambridgeshire and she knew the weather was similar even if it was the other way round. It would be warm summer there now – the prospect was very tempting. Her journey was uneventful although long and uncomfortable on the wooden seats in second class.

"I suppose I had better get used to it," she thought to herself.

When she arrived at Kings Cross it was the usual chaos and confusion of hundreds of people all going in different directions and horses pushing their way through the busy streets. It seemed even more chaotic than the last time she was home if that was possible, but she was able to stop and buy a newspaper with a similar advert to the one she had seen before. The prices were going up all the time. However, this advert said the price for a second class passage was still £15. If she were going to do it then she should do so before the prices increased any more.

London, she thought, amid the chaos, had a charm all of its own though and she loved hearing the costermongers cry competing with the sound of the trains and the general hubbub of daily life in the metropolis.

She boarded the horse drawn bus and giggled to herself as they overtook a horseless carriage that looked like a tin box on wheels. The maximum speed for these contraptions was only four miles an hour. She couldn't for the life of her see what they were bothering for because it was much quicker by horse. Mind you, the horses could be very smelly at times and one had to lift ones skirts up above the ankles to avoid getting a putrid mess around the hem.

All the time on the journey she had her mind focussed on how she was going to broach the subject of going to New Zealand. She, for a minute, even doubted herself.

"I must be mad" she told herself, "I have a lovely family and I have nothing to run away from." Then she thought again, "but I am nearly twenty five, I am responsible for myself now and I have nothing to stop me either." And so it was that she argued with herself all the way home. By the time she reached the door of her parent's house in Crichton Street it was going dark and the lamplighter was on his way round. In the distance she could hear the rumble of the newly built underground train but that didn't matter. She banged on the door and her father was there to greet her with open arms. She deftly tucked the newspaper into her big carpet bag.

"Welcome home, Charlotte my dear, we have all missed you."

She hugged her father and within minutes the rest of the family were crowded round – at least those that still lived at home. Her mother was closely followed by the teenagers, Amy, Fanny and Alice with little Annie running along behind.

"My Alice, haven't you grown big since I have been away?" smiled Charlotte, "and Thomas too!" She looked across at Thomas as he came out of his room where he had been making paper chains. He was starting to grow away too, he was almost as tall as his father.

"Come on, come on, make way" Their mother shooed them all off. "Let the girl get her coat off – I've some soup on the stove for you dear."

How could she bring herself to say that she wanted to emigrate? She felt more awful by the minute. Her mother had already prepared the Christmas dinner ready for tomorrow and she could see the turkey all trussed and stuffed and ready for the oven. She could imagine that she would be quite pleased to at least have the four older girls off hand. She knew she would be if it were her! She may have got the same name as her mother but she could not imagine herself being able to cope the same. She sampled the warm soup. It was lovely, as only her mother could make. She resolved that she would put off telling them of her plans until after the festivities. The two youngest children,

Thomas and Annie already had their stockings hanging by the kitchen range all ready for Father Christmas, Charlotte had knitted mittens for all her family during the time she had been in Cambridge and she had them tucked away in her bag all ready for the morning.

"Come on, lets get the paper chains up all ready for Father Christmas," said Thomas. He clapped his hands together, "Come on now children, or he will pass this house by."

They had made heaps of paper chains all out of strips of coloured paper pasted together with glue made out of flour and water. It wasn't very successful glue because they kept getting unstuck, but between them all they managed to cascade it around the room and out into the front porch.

"There!" exclaimed Thomas triumphantly as he put his arm round his wife. "Father Christmas should be happy with that."

It was soon time for the younger ones to go to bed and then the older sisters gathered around the fire and exchanged stories. The oldest in the little group, Amy, worked as a Kitchen Maid over at Kensington and she was sweet on the young boy that worked in the gardens.

"Plenty of time for you yet," said Mother, she picked up her sewing that had been discarded when her daughter arrived home. "You are only sixteen, don't be in too much of a hurry." She laughed out loud. "After all, look what happened to me!" She gestured towards the girls and then looked down at her ample figure. "It's hard work having a big family you know."

Charlotte couldn't help but think that it might be divine providence that she had not met a suitable beau yet. The later she started having babies then the less she would be likely to have to cope with. Her poor mother, like so many, seemed to have been having babies on an annual basis. Now, thankfully, she was too old to have any more. There were nine children but that did not count the others she had lost in childbirth, and she had been in her late forties by the time five year old Annie was born. Charlotte wanted a nice husband and children, of course, but not that many. In fact they were very lucky that Annie had been sound in mind and body. There were so many people having children late in life and it didn't always work out as it had for the baby of this family. She could remember the audible sighs of relief when her little sister was born and they found that she was all right.

"All the talk at school is about the immigration to New Zealand," said fourteen year old Fanny. "We have been learning all about it in geography."

Charlotte tried hard not to say anything, and just bit her lip. She would have to say something by tomorrow. She was going back to Cambridge the next day.

"I don't like geography" said Alice, "I like painting best."

"What about you Charlotte? What has been going on at Brownlow Mansions?"

"Well, I burnt the ham, .. well actually I didn't burn the ham – Sam did, but it was my responsibility and I did your trick with the breadcrumbs mother, and nobody knew any different." They all burst into peels of laughter.

"See I taught you well daughter, you will make a good cook."

Charlotte could hold it in no longer. She heard herself suddenly saying,

"That's what I want to be mother, but in New Zealand as an immigrant."

Everybody stopped their chat and Mrs. Adshead stood like a statue as if struck by some form of magic as Charlotte produced the newspaper from her bag.

Thomas Adshead was in the front room still finishing off some important tailoring for one of his special customers. It was a nice smart jacket and he was busy concentrating on setting in the sleeves when he heard the babble of noise suddenly stop. He poked his head around the door only to see his wife standing like a statue her sewing forgotten for the minute, and the girls sitting open mouthed staring at Charlotte. It was Amy that broke the silence.

"She wants to go off to the other side of the world father."

"Don't be foolish my girl," he chided "stop playing games, it costs a lot of money to go all that way."

"I would go on an assisted passage, and I already have ten pounds saved up. I just need another five."

His wife finally gathered her composure. Well this was a fine Christmas present their daughter had brought home. She was the first to realise what the girl was saying.

"So" she replied, "not only are you about to go off and leave us and probably never see us again, but you also want your father to help you to pay for it.?"

"Well I was hoping he might" said Charlotte, "After all you haven't had to pay for a dowry for me and this could be instead of that."

"You have got it all worked out haven't you child." said Thomas as he looked at the article in the newspaper which was now lying open on the table.

"And mother, I wouldn't be gone for ever. The new ships can get there in less than two months.

"Yes, across the boiling hot equator and some very dangerous seas!" piped up Fanny. "We learnt all about it in school."

Charlotte ignored her younger sister and what she had learnt about in school.

"Mother, look at me, I am twenty-five in a few days time. I am single and I need to have an adventure before it is too late. Why should the men have all the adventures and not the ladies – why, the ladies can not even vote for our Prime Minister?"

"And rightly so" grunted Thomas "that's just it, because they are ladies."

"Besides, I don't want to be a Parlour Maid for ever," she continued, "I want promotion and I am not going to get that at the Brownlow's. I want to be a cook."

Her mother fell about laughing.

"What after you have just finished telling me you burnt the ham?"

However, she felt some sympathy for her daughter. She too had wanted adventure some thirty or more years ago. She had been born down in Wiltshire and she too had been headstrong and had travelled up to London on her own to seek her fortune and, hopefully, a husband. She remembered the conversation with her parents then, and it was very similar to the one that was going on now. But this was hardly London. This was the other side of the world, although at the time London may have seemed like the other side of the world to her parents and grandparents.

"I made the ham good though," Charlotte said pointedly, "and everybody enjoyed it."

It could be seen that she was determined and all three of her sisters were starting to cry.

"Oh gawd! I wish I hadn't said anything now," said Charlotte, "I was going to leave it until tomorrow."

Thomas grunted again, scratched his balding head, and went back to his sewing. He didn't like to admit it, but he always had a soft spot for his second daughter out of all of his girls. She was the one named after his beloved wife, and she was the one with all the headstrong qualities that he so admired. He already knew deep down that he was going to give her the five pounds. Besides, although everyone made fun, she actually could cook very well and she could sew.

"Come on now girls." Their mother put some hot chocolate on the table for them. Stop these tears, it is not the end of the world."

"But she is going to the end of the world!" retorted Amy.

"No I'm not." Charlotte snapped, "I will be back one day and I promise I will write to you."

"Huh", tutted Alice "By the time we get the letter your news will be two months old."

"Come on" cried Mother, "It is Christmas soon and the younger ones will be up before you know it. – get yourself off to bed." She shooed them out of the room and there was just her and Charlotte left. She put an arm around her daughter.

"Don't worry, I'll talk to him – if it's what you want to do, we are in no position to stop you and if we don't give you the five pounds you will just save it up and will still go eventually."

"Or go steerage."

Mrs. Adshead grimaced, she wasn't having that, and she knew that Thomas would not hear of such a thing either. Steerage was the most uncomfortable way to travel on a very uncomfortable journey at the best of times. Everybody knew that.

Charlotte gave her mother a big hug and then went into the front room where her father was still stitching. She always admired his handiwork and was grateful to him for teaching her so much. It meant that she could turn her hand to anything. She certainly would not be out of work in New Zealand even if she couldn't get a job as a cook.

"I'm sorry if I upset you father." she said as she put her arm around his shoulder.

"It's the dangers my daughter," he replied without looking up from the machining he was doing. "There are still natives in that place, and it is fear of the unknown."

"The natives are Maoris father" and they are quite harmless. She watched him in admiration as he deftly continued to sew a fancy jacket and then put it with the rest of the orders on the rack. Most of the time he did all of the sewing himself but occasionally he had an apprentice tailor or help from any one of the girls. He fell silent but she continued to sit with him and sorted out his needles and cotton for him. The silence seemed to last for ever and then suddenly he drew a deep breath and stroked his beard.

"Well my girl, if you are determined on this then I will help you but it will only be once I have found out more about it. I have read about the Immigration policies in the paper but never thought it would affect any of my girls. If you are going to go it has to be done properly and on a decent ship – not some old bone shaker."

She flung her arms around him and hugged him.

"Honestly" she cried. "I will come home again one day, I promise,"

"Don't count your chickens my girl, you are not there yet," he grunted.

She gave him a kiss and ran back to her mother.

"He said yes" she laughed, "isn't it exciting!"

Amy came through from the bedroom just in time to hear the excitement, and burst into tears when she realised that her sister's departure for New Zealand seemed to be getting a real possibility. Mother felt it was time to call a stop to all the nonsense and get on with Christmas. Little Annie and young Thomas would be awake soon enough and they will be expecting Father Christmas to have been.

"Come on, that's enough of all this stuff and nonsense," she cried, "Enough, enough, enough, get yourselves off to bed. I've got stockings to fill up, this dress to finish and a plum pudding to make, all before the morning." Then as an afterthought, "Charlotte, you shall cook the turkey and Amy can prepare the vegetables tomorrow. If you are going to be a cook you had better get some practice in."

The two girls hurried off to get ready for bed, Amy to the big room that she was sharing with her other sisters and Charlotte to the room where Annie was sound asleep blissfully waiting for Father Christmas. Neither of them saw their mother brush away a tear.

The following day it was like every Christmas Charlotte had ever known. She had felt very lucky that once again her employers had given her substantial time off. She knew she would have to make up for it when she went back to Cambridge, but she was having nearly three days which was unheard of in the world of domestic servants. Once again she felt like an ungrateful wretch to be planning on giving up a job that most young ladies would have been very glad of.

Father Christmas had been good to everybody and little Annie and young Thomas opened their stockings gleefully. There was a real dolly with hand made clothes on for the baby of the family and Thomas had a wooden train just like the one that Charlotte went to Cambridge on, all made lovingly by their industrious parents. They had also bought or made things for each other and it was a happy time. There was a visit from older sister Julia, and her husband Wilfred, and everyone sang carols as the snow started to come down outside. It didn't matter to them as they were nice and warm by the kitchen range, with the turkey sizzling away inside. All the talk was about Charlotte and her plans to go to the other side of the world.

"Well I take my hat off to you," said Julia, "I don't think I would do it."

"Nor I" said Millie. "I'm sure I would be thoroughly sick on all those rough seas."

They all mucked in together and then in no time the dinner was on the table and Thomas said grace.

"For what we are about to receive may the Lord make us truly thankful."

Not for the first time Charlotte felt as though every word was aimed at her, and it certainly did not seem like a year since the original seed had been sewn when she ironed the newspaper at the Brownlows.

After dinner they all sang while Mother played the piano for them. All too soon the time came for Julia and Wilfred to leave and Thomas escorted them to the front door and flagged them down a carriage as everyone gathered around to wave them off. At the same time a horseless carriage stuttered past with a man walking in front of it. Another man was sitting up high in the driver's seat muffled up in hat and scarves and big top coat. It was spluttering and making the most peculiar noises. They all burst into peels of laughter as Julia lifted her skirts to get in her vehicle.

"It will never catch on" chortled Thomas, "look at that thing, how slow it goes."

Fortunately the driver couldn't hear them and went on his merry way unaware of the merriment that he had left behind in the doorway of 10 Crichton Street.

Christmas day passed very quickly and the girls amused themselves by rolling up each others hair and trying out the latest styles. One by one they got ready for bed and Charlotte was painfully aware that this might possibly be the last Christmas she would have with her large family for some years to come. In the morning she must go back to Cambridge and break the news to Augustus Brownlow that he was going to lose one of his parlour maids. But first she would need to call at the Immigration Office in Cambridge.

It was very early in the morning of Boxing Day that Charlotte packed her bag and got ready to go back to her place of work. There was just time for a big bowl of porridge and hugs from her family and, once again, Thomas went out to the front of the house to flag down a carriage for one of his daughter's. Suddenly he began to feel very old!

She gave him a squeeze and kissed his cheek.

"Thank you father for being so understanding," she said.

"Hmm!" he grunted. "You are not on the ship yet my girl – I need to satisfy myself that you know what you are doing."

"I do father, I do" I shall go to the Immigration Office but it is my belief that a ship called the British King is leaving for New Zealand in March and I hope to be on it."

Her mother wiped away a tear and gave her another hug.

"You take care" she said. "Take care on this journey on the train all the way to Cambridgeshire, never mind the three thousand or so miles to New Zealand!" She choked at the very thought and had to wipe away another tear.

Charlotte climbed into the carriage and waved goodbye. It was back to work, probably for the last time.

It was late afternoon when she arrived back at the mansion and Susan was waiting for her in her room. Now it was her turn to go home and Charlotte would take on the extra work to enable her friend to have some time with her family. Susan was, however, very anxious to find out how her friend had got on with confronting her family with the news of her future plans.

"Come on, tell all, what did your father and mother say?"

"Well they were not very pleased at first Susan, but..." she giggled knowingly, "I think I have won them round, in any case I am of age, so I can go if I want to."

"You are brave," replied Susan, "it's not for me."

She picked up her bag and made for the door.

"Anyway, you had better hurry up and get changed, his Lordship will be back tomorrow and you still have to tell Mrs. Catchpole and John."

"I'll wait until I am sure I have got a passage" said Charlotte, "I'd like to go in March – I believe that is the best time to travel."

Susan was none the wiser. All she knew was that she wouldn't do it.

❖ ❖ ❖

4. The Adventure Begins

Charlotte stood on the promenade deck of the SS British King and watched the coast of Plymouth slowly disappear into the distance. It was a lovely spring day and she was feeling more than a little bit nervous.

When she told her employers of her plans they had been at first, incredulous, and then very supportive.

"Well done, that girl," boomed Augustus when he had taken in the news relayed to him by Cook. "a young girl with a bit of spirit, that's what I like to see."

"It's mad if you ask me," muttered Mrs. Catchpole upon arrival back at the kitchen. "The whole world is going mad. If the lord had meant us to go to the other side of the world he would have given us wings."

She had gone to the Immigration Office in Cambridge on her first morning off and, with good references from the Brownlows, there was promise of a job as a Cook in a small settlement called Christchurch in the district of Canterbury on South Island, New Zealand, and she would have a berth on the steel hulled 'British King' The names Christchurch and Canterbury seemed rather comforting and she wondered whether they would be similar to their namesakes in Britain.

Her father had wanted to come with her all the way to Plymouth but she refused because she knew that, despite her excitement, she would still be very emotional and if she was going to have goodbyes it would be at the train station in

London so that she had time to gather her composure before going on board.

And so it was that the entire family escorted her to Paddington where she would get the train to the Devon coast and be ready for the sailing of the great ship. Even now, as she thought of all the hugs and the promises to write and then leaning out of the train carriage and waving until they were just dots in the distance – even now, she felt guilty at her single mindedness and she felt a great desire to burst into floods of tears.

"But then, nobody got anywhere without being single minded," she told herself and pulled herself together.

She had travelled down to Plymouth the day before and stayed in a hostelry overnight. The vessel wasn't due to depart until 3 pm but she didn't want to take any chances of the train being delayed on its long journey from London. She awoke early and was just in time to see the huge ship built by Harland and Wolff arrive in port at daybreak. It looked huge against the blue spring sky and its four hundred and ten foot length was awe inspiring. It seemed to sit low in the water because it was so heavy with produce and equipment that had been previously loaded in London.

It seemed to take hours to moor along side with the help of the pilot vessels, but then finally, along with, nearly three hundred other souls, she had her papers checked and all that remained was to go aboard. There was no turning back now.

The SS British King left the Royal Albert Docks in London, fully laden with all its supplies, on Thursday 13th March and travelled down the Thames, dropping anchor at the lower light ship to await the tide. Then escorted by the pilot ship from Deal she manoeuvred her way along the Channel with Captain Kelly in charge, arriving in Plymouth at daybreak on the 15th March ready to pick up her passengers including Charlotte.

She edged her way up the gangplank and was directed by one of the crew to the second class cabins for single girls. They were simple to say the least, just six bunk beds, three either side and made of wood with a thin mattress and a pile of blankets. Outside the door was a locker where they could store their bags. Not that anyone had much as there were very little in the way of washing facilities, and so most people knew that they would be in the same clothes for most of the journey.

"Well if this is second class I can't think what steerage must be like," she thought to herself.

Two girls had already arrived ahead of her. They both looked the same age as her and both had bagged the bottom bunks. They introduced themselves as Harriet and Emily.

"Pleased to meet you," said Charlotte politely and quickly learned that they were both aged 20 and that one came from Hampshire and the other from Surrey.

"I don't think I will be stopping in here very long on the voyage" said Harriet, "I'll be going up on deck to see what is going on."

"Oh we'll see about that" replied Emily, "You wait until we right get out to sea. You may think different then."

Charlotte quickly bagged the middle bunk and was just in time as, with lots of laughter and excited chat, the other three inhabitants of the cabin arrived and fell about in their efforts to claim their beds. It was soon established that they were from Galway in Ireland and were Anne O'Connor and two sisters Bridget and Catherine O'Brian aged twenty-two and eighteen. At nearly twenty-five Charlotte felt like the 'grannie' of the group.

Suddenly the engines took on a different tone and there was a shudder throughout the ship. There was plenty of time to find out more about her fellow passengers. Just now all she wanted to do was get up on deck so that she could see the ship leave port.

They all bumped into each other as they jumped down from the bunks. It was all going to take a lot of getting used to.

The girls ran up the steps and edged their way through the crowd to the ships rail just in time to see the shoreline move as the great vessel pulled away and crowds of people waved to their loved ones. Even now Charlotte felt very tearful and was glad that she had put the family off from the journey down to Plymouth.

Soon the ship was picking its way among the numerous other craft as it was skilfully guided out of harbour by the pilot ship.

"My word, it is almost as crowded as the streets of London!" she said out loud as she watched all the activity on the water.

"Exciting though isn't it" said a young boy of about ten who was standing on the rail, supported by his father and almost falling over the edge. "We are going to a whole new world." Charlotte secretly wondered what this whole new world would be like and what would lay in store for her at Christchurch, New Zealand.

"Well, next stop Tenerife" said Bridget excitedly in her soft Irish accent.

That was five days away. Just now everyone wanted to watch as the coastline of Britain slipped away into the distance and the pilot ship that had escorted them through the busy shipping lanes left them on their own. The British King gave a blast on her horns and the smaller vessel turned and made its way back to shore.

The girls were under no illusions. The journey would be rough and uncomfortable. It was pointless having too many clothes as there was very little facility for washing them. They soon realised that they would just have to remain in the same dress for most of the duration. Charlotte decided that she would keep one dress unused so that she had something decent to put on when she arrived at her destination in New Zealand. However, at the moment, the excitement of it all outweighed the possibility of having to stay in the same clothing for nearly two months.

The voyage was actually quite pleasant in the late Spring sunshine but 'needs must' and it was soon time to go down and find the galley and something to eat. Not that anyone felt like very much – even crossing these comparatively calm waters needed some getting used to.

The girls got ready as best they could and helped each other do their hair in the fashion of the day which was rolled up around their head. Only eighteen year old Catherine kept her blonde hair loose around her shoulders. Suddenly there was a cry from Harriet and the other three jumped out of their skins in fright.

Oh good lord a rat!" she screamed.

Charlotte was just in time to see the thing scurrying out of the door and under one of the luggage compartments outside.

"Gawd Harriet" she gasped, "you frightened me to bloody death!"

"I don't suppose for a minute that is the last creature we will see on board," said Emily, "I hope they have got a good ship's cat."

Emily was right of course. Before the end of the voyage they would come across any number of rats, and a goodly array of other objectionable creepy crawlies. Charlotte decided that she would stay up on deck as much as she could. After all, there was always a chance that she might meet a nice young man who could dispose of any rat that the ship's cat had overlooked!

❖ ❖ ❖

By the time they arrived at Tenerife to take on more coal, the girls had got to know each other. The three Irish girls were together trying to escape an impoverished life and do better for themselves. Harriet was a tall, very pretty girl with auburn hair who, like Charlotte, was out for adventure and a new life and chose New Zealand because she had been told that the climate and the scenery were similar to Britain. She also made it very clear that she was on the lookout for a rich husband. Emily was just twenty and desired to be a Lady's Maid.

"Well" thought Charlotte to herself when she tried to get ready for bed on their first night at sea, "we had better get on together, if we are going to live like this for the next few weeks."

They didn't disembark at this first port of call. Everyone came up on deck to see the extra coal being loaded and enjoy the evening sunshine. It was now very much warmer than they had experienced in Britain. All the first class passengers tended to stay at the front of the ship and on the Promenade Deck, where the second class people had their own areas. At least it wasn't steerage. Charlotte had seen the steerage quarters and people were squashed in and even more crowded down in the bowels of the great vessel. Provided the second class bunks were only used for sleeping and you could get out on deck it wasn't half bad. But it was early days yet. They left for the next stage of the journey the following morning. Now it would be seventeen days at sea.

❖ ❖ ❖

The journey was pleasant as far as Cape Town off the southern most tip of Africa. Pleasant, but very, very boring. They spent most of the time on deck just looking at the vast expanse of ocean all around them. It was a time to chat to the other passengers or to play guessing games. Charlotte tried to do a bit of washing in the basins provided and took advantage of the extremely hot weather and southerly wind to dry it. It was embarrassing though – she had not bargained for having to hang her bloomers on display. Moreover, she was forced to sit and guard them in case they blew away or were pinched by some wag wanting to have a joke.

"Gosh, we are becoming a stinky lot" said Harriet as she followed Charlotte's example but it had to be done and pretty soon there were a row of drawers and stays on a makeshift line. What the Captain and crew thought of it nobody ever knew. However, this practice was temporarily halted as they soon encountered thick fog and most people stayed below decks.

After what seemed to be a never ending journey the ship pulled in to Cape Town on 7th April 1884. By now Charlotte's birthday had been and gone and she was now officially twenty-five.

The ship was to spend the entire day taking on more coal and would be there a further day after that so there was a chance to go ashore for those who were brave enough.

Captain Kelly made it clear that the shipping company would not be responsible for anybody who went ashore and advised any ladies to be accompanied by a man. The six girls were determined to go and soon found some worthy gentlemen that they had got to know on the voyage to escort them.

"After all" said Bridget, "I'm sure they won't mind, they have even seen our bloomers."

It passed Charlotte's mind that her parents would have a fit if they knew the goings on, especially as most of the women and children did, in fact, remain on board.

Charlotte marvelled at the fine houses with the wide streets, and they even had a train running through it, but here the similarity to Britain ended.

"Oh my God, look at them" whispered Harriet.

"Don't point" said Charlotte "it's rude."

She had seen a few black people before in London, but never dressed like this and for the rest of the girls it was a most unusual sight. The women with their gaily coloured dresses that showed off their legs and huge headdresses and everyone, male and female wore some really strange looking shoes that were just soles with the toe through a strap that came up between the big toe and second toe, almost defying the laws of gravity. The men were wearing some strange looking grass hats that shaded their eyes from the sun, similar to those that Chinamen wore. Albert, who was one of the men that the girls were clinging to asked how much one of the hats would cost to buy and got told £1.

"One pound!" gasped Harriet "One pound – I don't think so."

"Come on" said Albert, "they are trying to pull a fast one."

They all walked along together and noted the prices of some of the goods on display for the passengers to buy. Everything was double the price of the same article at home.

"Look at that" said Harry, "Cheese is 1/6d a pound, that's extortion!"

"And look" added Charlotte, "a shilling for jam."

Harriet shuffled around in her purse and paid over a shilling.

"Let's buy a pot between us" she said, "the rolls we get for our meals will be better for it."

Charlotte decided again that her mother would be horrified, but they bought their jam and eventually made their way back to the ship where it was infinitely safer.

They set sail the following morning and then word went around the second class passengers that three stowaways had been found hiding until the ship had got too far from land for anything to be done about them. It was too late to turn the ship around and so they were put to work to pay for their passage, scrubbing the decks and fetching and carrying food from the galley to the crew.

It would now be another three weeks before they would see the coast of Tasmania on their journey to their first port of call which would be Auckland, and already the weather was turning colder. A few days later and they were in the teeth of a gale that lasted for four days. People were sick and it was a nightmare, and at the same time funny trying to eat at the table in the galley with the boat rocking from side to side. If you were on the wrong side of the ship the waves came in and enveloped them and rolled them across the deck to the other side causing a few injuries and completely soaking them through. The only way to dry clothes now was at the stoke hole if you were lucky enough to get to know one of the crew.

Most of the time the six girls stayed on their bunks in their cabin, but for the two on the topmost bunks it was very precarious as the ship, despite its size, rocked on the waves and threw them from side to side.

All merriment on the ship ceased when news came of the death of a youngster. A little boy aged five who had developed some illness that the ships doctor could not treat. There was nothing for it but to consign him to the deep. Those that could went up on deck and braved the weather and a shudder went all around as they watched the body, wrapped in a sheet, slide off the board into the water and heard the wails of the mother as she fell to the floor in a heap. The father stood by the rail and had the face of one who was living a nightmare which he would like to wake up from. This experience sobered everyone up for the rest of the journey but the excitement gradually returned when they became aware that the ship was approaching land At eleven o'clock on the night of 2nd May the vessel pulled into Auckland Harbour.

Of course it was winter in this part of the world and everywhere was pitch black but Charlotte heard the sound of a dog barking and it was a welcome sound indeed.

"Listen to that" said Harriet, "civilisation!"

This was where some of the passengers were disembarking including Anne, Bridget and Catherine, the three Irish girls. For Harriet, Emily and Charlotte there were still more days at sea, along with seventy or so others, many of whom were Scots.

The following morning Charlotte stood on deck and looked at the neat houses around the quayside, mostly painted in a stone colour and set wide apart with plenty of land to each with large trees all around. The doctor came aboard and examined all the passengers that were disembarking and the Immigration Officer gave them their papers. Anne, Bridget and Catherine, like most of the women, changed into the dresses that they had been saving throughout the voyage.

Catherine held her old one up between her thumb and forefinger as if it was some smelly rag, which it almost was.

"Begorra that is so stinky," she cried. "I'll be glad to just throw it away."

All that remained then was for the girls to give each other a hug and the three joined the other passengers going ashore. What lay ahead of them in this new world, nobody knew.

"Take care!" shouted Harriet, "have a good life."

Then they were gone, lost in the crowd.

The ship was due to stay in port for a couple of days to re-stock with provisions and coal so three girls who were left went ashore to see the shops.

"Look how neat and tidy everywhere is," said Harriet

"Ooh look!" exclaimed Emily, "the Post Office looks no different from ours at home."

"Well it would look the same silly," said Charlotte, "most people here are British anyway – everyone said it would be a home from home."

As if to defy what she had just said a group of Maori men stood huddled together on the quayside, smoking pipes and watching the activities. The girls had all seen pictures of them in magazines and believed them to be friendly, but it was quite a shock to see them in real life with their skirts and painted flesh.

They gave them a wide berth and then spent some time looking around the shops. They found that, generally speaking, the clothes were cheaper than in England.

It gave them a chance to stock up on scarves and gloves for the forthcoming New Zealand winter, especially as they knew that the South Island was going to be altogether colder.

Meat was the cheapest of all. There was a huge shop called the Gear Refrigerating Company who exported lamb all over the world and the carcasses were hanging up in the shop window like rows of rabbits would have been at home. A half leg of lamb could be bought for fourpence.

"I think I am going to like it here," said Emily.

But their journey was by no means over. They had to traverse the whole country to get to their final destination of Lyttleton Harbour in the district of Canterbury, calling at Wellington and Hawkes Bay on the way. They left Auckland on 5th May for a journey that should only have lasted thirty-six hours. Instead it lasted five days. The wind was so rough and the ship was heading straight into it and was tossed around like a cork. It was worse than anything they had experienced around the Cape. The three girls were glad that with the others gone they had more room in the cabin and they huddled together on the bottom bunks.

Never were they so glad to arrive anywhere than Wellington Harbour where, once again, more of the passengers would be disembarking.

"Not many of us now" said Emily when they went to the galley and tried to eat something. It was the first they had for days and now that the ship had come to rest they were glad of it.

They were able to go ashore at this busy capital city for a little while and looked around at all the wooden buildings whilst more stores were loaded on the ship. Even the Government Building was made of wood, the largest wooden building in the country, and to the back of that was the big penal colony.

"Its not just Australia that has the convicts then," observed Emily, "it looks like New Zealand has its fair share."

Charlotte thought they were taking a bit of a chance with the buildings being made of wood. There would not be much hope in the case of fire. However, it was very grand with cream coloured walls and bright red tiled roofing and standing in its own grounds amid beautifully kept lawns. It all looked very bright and majestic in the sunshine. It was good to look around

The Tailor's Daughter ~ 47

at this fast growing city built against a backdrop of mountains, but really all she wanted now was to get some clothes washed and be respectable for the arrival at their final destination.

Eventually, she got her wish and after a short stop at Hawke's Bay at the north of South Island, they finally pulled in to Lyttleton Harbour in the district of Canterbury on the 17th May 1884. The girls hugged each other and laughed and cried at the same time.

"I wonder what will befall us now," said Harriet.

Charlotte wondered too. She didn't know where she would be living or who she would be working for. She just knew that she had put herself down to be a cook and had good references from her previous employer, and she had a clean dress.

Seventy-two people disembarked at Lyttleton Harbour and most of them were to stay in hostels at the Government's expense until an employer was found.

The harbour was enclosed on three sides by high hills and the scenery was breathtaking.

"It looks like bonnie Scotland" whispered a voice nearby, "just like the hills around Loch Lomond."

They were met by some elderly looking officials and shown to their accommodation. A tubby business like little man checked their papers.

"You all get used to being ashore now," he said. "We'll sort out employment for you tomorrow."

Then Captain Kelly joined them and shook the hands of as many people as he could.

"The British King is going to be anchored here for the next week, to take on tons of lamb bound for England. If you want to write home I suggest you do it within the next few days and we'll deliver it for you."

SS British King

It seemed strange to be actually on land and living in a room that wasn't moving. Within twenty four hours of their arrival they were visited by the Minister of Emigration, a large pleasant looking man who welcomed them to New Zealand. Most of the Cooks jobs were, as at home, for the gentry and he soon found a placement for Emily as a Parlour Maid.

"I have a variety of cooks jobs here" he informed Charlotte, "mostly for the gentry, and there is also one for the 'Sailor's Return'." He said that one almost as an afterthought, as if he didn't think she would be interested. Charlotte, on the other hand, was very interested. It sounded like something new and she had not come all this way to do more of the same.

"Sailors' Return,"? she queried.

"Yes, it's the hostelry just up the hill here for when the sailors are in port. Its run by Mr. and Mrs. Braithwaite . You can go for an interview if you like, but remember, you can't turn down too many positions, otherwise you have to take the last one offered."

The Tailor's Daughter ~ 49

Harriet and Emily seemed to be settled with their future employers so Charlotte arranged to go and see what this 'Sailor's Return' was like. Clearly it was a Public House and she briefly wondered what her parents would think of that!

She didn't take much persuading. The following day she entered the large timbered building and met the Landlord and his wife. Both of them looked as though they enjoyed good food being large and jolly. She took to them straight away.

"Come in, come in my dear and welcome."

A group of sailors were sitting in the corner sampling the ale and she could smell the faint aroma of something cooking coming from the back. She had already decided that if they were happy with her then she would be happy with them. Besides, one never knew, this could be her chance of meeting gentlemen friends which would be less likely to happen if she were working for the gentry. It was six months since Charlotte had shocked her parents by saying that she wanted to emigrate, and now she was here and she had a job. Moreover, she had a nice little room of her own, the first time in her entire life. All that remained was to write home and they should get her letter before Christmas.

5. Introducing the Gosleys

James Morehouse Gosley and his crew steered the Pilot Ship Mary Jane into the harbour at Deal. He would be glad to get home as he had just spent the last day or so escorting the emigration ship 'British King' out of the Thames and around the Kent Coast before handing over the task to the 'Saucy Sal' who would escort it the rest of the way to Plymouth. He was sixty four now and it was a job he had been doing all his life. The sea was in his veins, passed on by his father, grandfather and even his great grandfather who was going to sea at the time of George the first. It was also in the veins of his three sons, James, Frederick and Francis. James was in the Navy, Frederick was a Merchant Seaman and the youngest, Francis, had married and settled down in New Zealand working in HM Customs. Or he had, until very recently! He felt a lump come to his throat when he thought of young Francis, or Frank as everyone called him. The poor lad had gone blind! It was such a crying shame. James had been so proud of him when he got his certificate to be a First Mate on the merchant ships along with his brother. Then, whilst on a trip to New Zealand he met the love of his life, Andria, who came from Scotland. He settled down with her five years ago and got a position with HM Customs so that he could be with her and not be away for years on end. Then, just when everything had been going so swimmingly for the couple, be had gone blind! He was not yet thirty years old. It seemed that nothing could be done in New Zealand and so he was advised to come back to England and go to the Moorfields Eye Hospital to see what they could do for him. His parents were devastated.

Of course, James, who was financially quite successful, being the owner of his own boat, paid for Francis to go to the famous Hospital in London but to no avail. Now the young couple were staying with his daughter, young Jane and her husband, whilst training to be a piano tuner. Despite the ache in his heart James Morehouse Gosley smiled to himself. It was a far cry from being the First Mate on a Merchant Ship! Of course it had been wonderful to see him again after five long years away, and to meet his pretty young Scottish wife, but he did not want it to be under those circumstances. It had been a bitter/sweet reunion.

"I would rather never see the lad again than have him endure this" he said to his wife.

Once again the house was empty. Empty that is, but for his wife Jane and their fifteen year old servant girl. They were beginning to rattle around in the four bedroom house in the posh part of Deal and he wondered where in the world his second son Frederick was. He could be anywhere!

His older boy James had long since left home and was married with a family of his own and even the youngest, Annie, was temporarily away working as a Parlour Maid.

That left Frederick who was just a couple of years older than Frank. Until 1879, the brothers had been inseparable. It had been such a shock when he learned of his brother's deteriorating eyesight.

"Don't you worry about me Freddy" Frank had said, "you go out and have your adventures and show them what us Gosleys are made of brother."

Now Frederick was half way round the world as First Mate on the Immigration ship, the SS British Empire and his ever patient parents did not really have a clue where he was.

James and Jane were used to their boys being away for years on end and this time it was no exception. He had left Plymouth a year ago and the family knew it was a case of 'wait and see' as far as he was concerned. All his father knew was that this Immigration bug was affecting everybody. Why, only today he had seen off the sister ship, the 'British King', on its journey to the Antipodes. He sent up a little prayer for them. He was happy just sticking to being a Cinque Port Pilot. The Channel was quite enough for him these days.

He checked that the men had moored the ship steadfastly and then strode down the road towards his house in Castle Terrace lost in his own thoughts.

He had been piloting ships round the Thames Estuary and Kent for as long as he could remember and taking immigrants out to Australia and New Zealand since the 1850s, but this new ship, the British King was the most impressive of them all. Having said that, he couldn't help but feel a bit of nostalgia for the passing of the majestic sailing ships.

It was only a few strides round to his house and, as always, Jane was there waiting for him with the stew pot on the go and her usual warm smile. Like him, she was in her sixties now, but she had not lost any of her beauty, and in his eyes anyway, she was as young as the day he met her. He kicked off his boots and sank down into his favourite chair. Young Emily, the servant girl, brought him his slippers and then waited to see what else was required of her. James couldn't help but think that they couldn't really justify keeping her now that the house was so empty.

Jane read his thoughts and as soon as Emily was out of earshot she voiced what he was thinking.

"We can't get rid of her James" she said, "bless her, she is only fifteen and has nowhere else to go."

This was true and there was really no answer to it.

"Well that's another lot on their way," he muttered, "God help them and God speed."

"I wonder where in the world Frederick is?" said Jane.

"Good question," laughed her husband, "he could be anywhere."

"It's about time he found himself a nice wife," replied Jane, "after all he is in his thirties now."

"Oh I am sure he will surprise us one of these days Jane, I'm sure he will surprise us my dear."

He twirled his bushy moustache and then scratched his thinning grey hair.

"It's Frank that has worried me," he mused, "I'll be happy once I know he is settled in a good position with his piano tuning."

"Well, the girls say he is managing it all right, so he might surprise us as well," said Jane "and he does have a very good steady wife in Andria."

James heaved himself out of the chair and went in the back scullery to wash his hands ready for dinner. He took his pocket watch out of his waistcoat which was stretched about his ample belly and noted the time.

"Look at that my dear, its eight o'clock and the sun is setting. It will be morning away in that far off place where that ship has gone to."

"No wonder they send the convicts there," Jane replied, "they couldn't send them any further away could they?"

He sat at the table and the smell from the stew that Emily dished up was heaven itself.

"Well the 'British Empire' was bound for New Zealand too, so I should think young Frederick will be there somewhere." He started to taste his lamb stew. "One thing I do know – apart from being somewhere to send the convicts that far off country does have its other uses – and that is their lamb."

❖ ❖ ❖

The SS British Empire with First Mate Frederick Gosley on board had sailed into Lyttleton Harbour a few days ahead of the British King and all the crew were having a well earned rest. It had been a rough crossing and, not for the first time, Frederick wondered why he had become a merchant seaman and not a Cinque Ports Pilot like his father. He knew his father experienced some rough seas but at least he didn't have to go round that bloomin' Bay of Biscay. It had flung everything at them on this journey.

Then he corrected himself. In fact the Channel ports could be just as tricky especially with the amount of traffic. He remembered very well the worry that the whole family went through when his father's ship had gone down in the Channel, struck by a vessel from Bermuda that had no right to be where it was. The whole crew of The Princess were consigned to the waves and two of them lost their lives. Thankfully father was saved, but it never put him off his job or of supporting his boys in their desires to follow in his footsteps.

There was a lot of work to be done on the ship after this latest voyage, restocking with coal and also with goods and mail to be delivered back in Britain. It was likely to take some weeks so many of the crew chose to go ashore and take advantage of the local hostelry. Some of the younger ones were also anxious to see if there were any young ladies to take their fancy.

"And they don't have to be too ladylike either" laughed young Simon Brown. "I'll take whatever is going!"

"Behave!" replied Frederick. He was responsible to the Captain for their behaviour and whilst he realised that they needed to let off steam, they were part of her Majesty's Merchant Navy. He had been here before and Lyttleton Harbour was not new to him.

"Come on Fred, leave them be." He felt a slap on the back and his best friend Andrew was at his side. "Let's go and pay a visit to the Braithwaite's at the 'Sailor's Return'. I think I would rather go there than spend any more time on this ship." Then as an afterthought he tapped his hand gently on the ships rail, "no offence meant old girl, no offence meant."

They were soon joined by some of the other older crew and, having made sure that the boat was secure and safe in the hands of the Harbour masters, the group of sailors made their way up the hill.

❖ ❖ ❖

Mrs. Braithwaite showed Charlotte around the Inn and introduced her to the rest of the staff. There was a pot man called Bert and two young ladies who, she said, 'did for her'. It soon became clear that, apart from cooking, she would be expected to take her turn in doing other necessary jobs, but it was a nice family atmosphere and the new arrival was won over completely. All that remained was to collect her bag from the hostel. She hadn't brought it with her as she didn't want to be presumptuous. After all, she didn't know whether she would be wanted or not, and she certainly didn't know what it would be like to work in a Tavern. She was about to find out.

The Sailor's Return was a large wooden building, painted white, and with the traditional Inn sign hanging from a support on the wall. It could have been from anywhere in Britain and even the road it was in was called London Road. Charlotte wondered about the sense of coming all that long way around the world, and risk gale and tempest, just to end up in a carbon copy of Britain! Even the Landlord and Landlady were like characters from Punch magazine. Both were heavily overweight and they came from Lancashire, but already she could see that they would be like parents to her. Jenny Braithwaite folded her arms across her ample bosom and peered at Charlotte.

"Mm, I expect you will want some new clothes. There are plenty of shops both here and in Christchurch with tailors that will soon run you up some dresses, but you can also use my sewing machine if you want to make your own."

That clinched it as far as Charlotte was concerned. To be let loose with a sewing machine was her idea of heaven, and she hadn't even asked what the wages were yet. Jenny Braithwaite read her mind.

"Twelve pounds a month and your keep – what do you say?" Then as an afterthought she added, "mind you, you had better be able to cook. You can prepare the dinners tomorrow and we'll see – no point in wasting any time."

"I say, thank you very much," laughed Charlotte. "I'll go and get my bags if I may?" The idea of preparing the dinners for the sailors did not worry her. She felt she'd had plenty of practice one way and another, despite the incident of the ham back at the Brownlow establishment.

The Tailor's Daughter ~ 57

James Braithwaite had been busy at the bar with the sailors but came over to welcome the new Cook. He was a rotund, florid faced man in his fifties.

"Welcome my lass, welcome." he boomed, "I hope you will be able to manage this motley crew and others like them."

She followed his gaze to where about half a dozen sailors were sitting in the corner chatting and drinking beer. She was particularly drawn to one older looking one, who looked to be in his early thirties. He had a kind face and a twinkle in his eye and his gaze met hers. She was long past giving men the 'glad eye' and, in any case, she really was not feeling at her best. She did need new clothes and she had lost weight on the voyage so that her dress was too big. Mind you, she wasn't complaining about that – always built on the heavy side, she certainly would not miss a few pounds. She had managed to get a bath at the hostel the night before so at least she was clean.

Frederick Gosley drew himself up from his chair and touched his forelock. He had the air of someone who was used to being obeyed and in control of things. He had a demeanour that was bordering upon arrogant, which Charlotte quite liked.

"Hello" he grinned "Things are looking up in this Tavern – the surroundings are more beautiful already."

Charlotte felt herself blush bright red. He clicked his heels together in mock subservience.

"Frederick Gosley at your service Madam!"

"Charlotte Adshead" she replied "I've just arrived from London.

"Oooh a cockney lass eh!

The other sailors seemed to be egging him on to make further advances but for some reason he did not. He just grinned and sat down again and finished his beer.

Jenny Braithwaite came to her rescue and got her husband out of the house, all in one fell swoop.

"James! Escort the young lady down to the hostel and help her with her baggage – come on man, stir your stumps."

One of the other sailors shouted out.

"Don't worry Charlotte! Fred isn't going anywhere, he will still be here when you return."

"Gawd!" she muttered under her breath.

She was even more embarrassed and glad to get back down the road to the hostel, ably escorted by her employer.

"I can see I am going to have to keep an eye on my staff," laughed James Braithwaite as they got out of earshot. "I'll be losing you to the crew of the British Empire."

"I don't think so!" Charlotte replied, "though I did like the older one."

"Frederick!" said James, "Oh Frederick is all right – we see him quite regularly when the ship is in port. His poor brother losing his eyesight knocked him back a bit and he is quieter these days."

"Oh?" Charlotte left the question hanging in the air.

"Yes, sad business, poor boy. Used to come in on the ships with his brother. The pair of them were inseparable. Then he lost his eyesight and that was the end of his career on the sea."

"Oh blimey" replied Charlotte, "that's awful."

They walked round the bend in the road going towards the quayside and were just in time to catch Harriet and Emily climbing on board a carriage bound for Christchurch and their new jobs. They all hugged each other.

"Goodbye" called Emily, "Christchurch is not very far, I'm sure we shall see each other before long."

"Goodbye Emily, goodbye Harriet, and good luck."

Charlotte wrapped her coat and shawl around herself as she watched them disappear up the road. At the same time the Time Ball in Lyttleton Harbour recorded that it was one o'clock. She shivered and almost wished she was at home in an English summer instead of a New Zealand winter and hearing about Frederick's blind brother. It wasn't hard to imagine that the next land across the sea from here was the Antarctic. She almost expected to see a penguin waddling along the road any minute from now.

James Braithwaite walked inside the hostel with her and sat in the waiting room while she went and picked up her bags. There wasn't a lot but it was heavy enough and she was glad of him to help her carry it up the hill. She couldn't help but feel that this new chapter of her life was really beginning and, despite her best efforts not to, she did find herself wondering if Frederick Gosley would still be at the Sailor's Return when she got back there.

It was good to have James carry her bags. He was a friendly chap although he stopped chatting for the want of breath as they made their way back up the hill.

"I wished I'd got the carriage out now" he puffed, "I'm not as fit as I thought."

Jenny was waiting for them and there was a healthy smell of hot pot coming from the kitchen. Charlotte tried to pretend she wasn't looking but she couldn't miss the group of sailors busy swapping yarns in the corner. Frederick Gosley looked up and gave her a wink. She smiled back and then followed her new employers through to the back.

"Come on, I'll show you where your room is – you can share with Edith. She is a nice child – a bit young but you'll find her useful in the kitchen. My other girl, Doris, lives with her parents and comes in each day to help out."

Edith was pinning her hair up as they knocked on the door. Charlotte saw a pretty girl with fair curls that were having a job staying in place despite her efforts.

"Hello" said Edith "I am sure we will get on famously."

"I'm sure we will" smiled Charlotte.

It was a smart and clean room and Charlotte could see that there was clean bedding. There was as much room as she would have had at home. She didn't think her mother would approve of her working in a Tavern but she was pleased with her choice.

"I think Frederick Gosley fancies you" said Edith when Jenny Braithwaite had left them, "I saw the way he was looking at you."

Charlotte laughed.

"Maybe he fancies you Edith," She couldn't have been a year older than eighteen.

"Nah – too old for me. He is thirty-one!"

She said it as if he was at least seventy.

"That old?" laughed Charlotte.

The next thing on her agenda was to write a letter home. It would go on the next ship out of the harbour and with a bit of luck be with her family before the Autumn.

Frederick was quite taken by the cockney girl who had just come to work for the Braithwaites. He had courted various young ladies in the past but as he was becoming older so the unattached girls were getting younger. He found Charlotte to be attractive and as she was nearer in age to him he felt a kindred spirit. He knew in his heart of hearts that he wanted to see more of her and found himself cursing the job that kept him away from loved ones for so long. He wondered if she would remain faithful when the 'British Empire' followed the 'British King'

The Tailor's Daughter ~ 61

and continued on its way in a weeks time. Indeed, he wondered if she would be attracted to him anyway. After all, she might not be.

He needn't have worried. Charlotte was having the same thoughts when she tucked herself in bed that night and said goodnight to Edith.

"I'm telling you, he was watching you all night" whispered Edith. "You may end up being the future Mrs. Gosley."

"Gawd Edith, don't be silly. I've only just met him." But she did have a nice warm feeling in the pit of her stomach when she turned over and pulled the blankets over her head. 'Mrs. Charlotte Gosley' – it had a nice sound to it.

By the end of the week, not only was she fast becoming well known for her excellent cooking she was well and truly hooked by Frederick Gosley. It didn't take her long to get used to all the kitchen equipment and, with Edith taking on the irksome task of preparing the vegetables, Charlotte was soon producing the best lamb stews in the area and Jenny and James were well satisfied with their new employee.

❖ ❖ ❖

6.   Happiness and Tragedy

It may have been Autumn in England but it was Spring in New Zealand and Charlotte also had a spring in her step as she busied herself doing her chores at the Sailor's Return.

Two months had passed since she first met Frederick Gosley and she knew that he was the man for her. Most of this time the SS British Empire had been in harbour having refits and overhauls and the crew spent each day getting her ready for her next voyage. There had been one trip where the ship had been away for a fortnight, travelling up to Auckland to pick up supplies and post, but generally speaking, during, what would be the winter months in the northern hemisphere, she stayed down south. There would be time enough next year to do the long haul trip back to England.

Now that the weather was changing for the better it was time to enjoy the breathtaking scenery in that part of New Zealand and she had the most perfect of escorts when Frederick had his days off. The time when he was away at sea seemed like 'for ever' to Charlotte. It was during these forced separations that she wrote home to tell her parents all about her new life.

❖ ❖ ❖

Back in England, both in Clapham and in Deal there were parents who were without their children that Christmas. Letters took two months to arrive at their destinations so the festive season was in full swing by the time the postman arrived at the Adshead household.

Everyone gathered round to hear Thomas read from Charlotte's letter enclosed with a parcel.

> "The scenery here is delightful and puts me in mind of pictures I have seen of Scotland. I'm working at a Tavern for a lovely northern couple called Mr. and Mrs Braithwaite and I get to do the cooking for the sailors who spend most of their time here. The Tavern is in London Road and overlooks the lovely harbour. Mrs Braithwaite lets me use her sewing machine and I have made several dresses since I have been here. I also hope you all like the woollen gloves I am enclosing. They are made from the wool from the backs of the sheep that roam in their thousands on the hills.
>
> We have seen little of the Maori population who seem to keep themselves to themselves but they are quite an awesome sight when gathered together on the street corners.
>
> Also I have met a lovely gentleman who is the First Mate on the British Empire. His name is Frederick and he comes from Kent. He is so kind and nice that I really think I might marry him one day."

"Ooooh!" piped up Amy and Fanny together. "Our Charlotte has found a gentleman friend."

"Wonders will never cease!" said Alice as she tried on the lovely wool gloves.

"What is she doing working in a Tavern though?" said Mother, "I thought she was going out there to work for the gentry."

"Well she seems happy enough," replied Thomas, "I can't ask for more than that for my daughters."

"I wonder what Frederick is like?" giggled Alice. "I wonder whether we will meet him one day."

❖ ❖ ❖

Over at Deal the Gosley family were kept wondering. They were used to their offspring being away from home and they were also used to having to wait a considerable amount of time for letters. They were more concerned at the moment about Francis. Things were beginning to turn a corner for him and he had passed his exams to be a piano tuner and Andria had stuck by him.

James and Jane Gosley greeted it all with mixed feelings. It was good that the boy had found a woman who would look after him and clearly did not worry about his blindness, but she was Scottish and they intended to go and live at her home town of Edinburgh.

"Such a long way off," said Jane, when Francis gave her the news. "Such a long way off Frank – we will miss you."

"Well it's not as far as Frederick mother," he replied. He looked at her with his unseeing eyes. "Transport is improving all the time – soon you will be able to get to Scotland in a couple of days."

He was right of course, and Jane could not help but feel relieved that her Frank had found such a good woman in Andria. Losing his eyesight had been such a blow and made more so because even the well reputed Moorfields Eye Hospital in London had not been able to help him. They said it was glaucoma, but it meant nothing if it could not be fixed. Moreover she felt just a little bit selfish. After all Andria had been away from home for years and her family were bound to be missing her.

"It would be nice to think that Frederick could get himself settled," said James. "It's time that boy got on with it or he will be too old."

"He's only thirty-one James," replied Jane, "plenty of time."

"Ten years older than I was wife – ten years older than I was!"

But still, he couldn't help but think that it would be sad for Fred to come home and find his brother had gone to Scotland, although he knew his elder son well. He, like the rest of the family would be glad that young Frank was getting his life on track again and they were used to long separations within the family.

❖ ❖ ❖

The New Zealand summer seemed to drift by all too quickly and Charlotte had to endure long stretches when Frederick was away with the ship, but the longest was to come. With the shipping routes opening up around the Bay of Biscay again the SS British Empire was ready to set sail for home carrying ten thousand carcasses of mutton. It meant that he would be away for at least four months.

"When I return we will get married," he assured her, and he slipped an engagement ring on to her finger to prove the point. It was too big but she could have it altered.

"My grandmother's," he explained. "I'll get you one of your own one day."

She was almost tempted to go with him – to call a day on her adventures in New Zealand, but Charlotte was not a quitter and she enjoyed working for the Braithwaites. She and Frederick had spent much of their time together making plans and those plans were based on a future in this new world. Of course, she would like to go home one day, but not yet. She made her mind up that she would use any spare time she had by visiting Harriet and Emily in Christchurch and she would sew clothes and bedding for her bottom drawer. If she kept herself busy the time would soon pass. She could write letters and keep diaries and go out and see the lovely scenery in this most beautiful part of New

Zealand. She could also try out some new recipes on the customers at the 'Sailor's Return'. She would cope.

Nevertheless she shed many a tear on the day the SS British Empire pulled out of Lyttleton Harbour bound for England.

She stood on the quayside and watched as the ship was loaded and the crew busied themselves preparing the vessel for departure. Finally Frederick appeared from below decks and came ashore to give her one last kiss amid cheers from his comrades.

"Don't forget" he whispered, "this time next year we will be married."

He looked round and made a rude gesture at Andrew and the rest of the crew who were hanging over the side of the ship egging him on.

"Take no notice of them," he grinned. "They are just jealous."

With that he went on board – a stocky figure in his sailor's uniform of dark blue trousers and thick jersey.

Charlotte went and sat on a bollard and waited until the ship began to pull away, first slowly and then picking up speed. She watched until it had rounded the corner at the end of the bay and was out of sight. In just over two months time he would be in England. He was carrying a letter for her parents and lots of news for his.

❖ ❖ ❖

The months that Frederick was away were interminable. Jenny and James Braithwaite kept her busy and she had fun dressmaking and making stuff for her bottom drawer but every day dragged by. It would be summer in England but it was coming up to winter again here in New Zealand. For the first time in a year she was beginning to wish she had stopped at

The Tailor's Daughter ~ 67

home, but then she would never have met Frederick. She paid a visit to see Harriet and Emily in Christchurch. Everywhere looked so new – even the Cathedral and it made her think of London and how different everything was. Not for the first time she wondered how Frederick would be received by her family.

"It's so exciting," giggled Harriet, "our Charlotte getting married at last."

"Oi! Enough of the 'at last' she retorted. "I'm not that old."

"Well, at least you won't have dozens of children to worry about," replied Emily, "I think it is good to be a late starter."

"If he doesn't come home soon I'll be lucky to get started at all!" grumbled Charlotte, and the conversation ended in girlish laughter.

❖ ❖ ❖

For Frederick it was the long arduous and sometimes dangerous journey that everyone expected. In fact for the first time in his life he had actually been seasick in the gales that they had encountered around the Cape. But as First Mate he had a responsibility to the passengers, many of whom were ill and so, along with the other hundred or so crew they battled against the elements for two months before finally arriving in the English Channel and the pilot ship came alongside to guide them the rest of the way. Frederick briefly wondered if it was his father at the helm but the Captain soon reassured him that it wasn't.

Most of the crew had shore leave and would be going by train or carriage to see their families, whilst some of the younger ones stayed in the Taverns around the Albert Docks and drunk themselves into oblivion.

Frederick had a job to do and any idea that he might have had of joining Andrew, and some of the others at the Tavern were put to one side as he put his bag on his back and hailed a carriage to take him to Clapham.

It took him some while to take in the cacophony of noise that echoed round the London streets in 1885. It was mostly horses and carriages but interspersed in between and causing total chaos were the horseless carriages.

They were strange looking objects with big wheels and they kicked up a noise and a degree of smoke that he had never seen before. He marvelled at the patience of most of the horses and wondered where it would all end. Would these contraptions take over on the London streets? It seemed hard to imagine when a team of horses could pull a bus along quite successfully.

The carriage drew up at Crichton Street and he paid the driver.

"Well done my man" he laughed, "I don't know how you cope with all this chaos."

"Practice guv', practice" answered the cabbie as he shook the reins and the horse and carriage trotted off.

Now, as Frederick knocked on the door of the Tailor's Shop belonging to Thomas Adshead, he suddenly felt nervous. Charlotte had told him all about her family so he knew mostly what to expect and he knew that she had written to them some months ago to tell them about the engagement, but it wasn't every day that he found himself knocking on the door of complete strangers knowing that he was going to ask for their daughter's hand in marriage.

The door was opened by young Alice who was now thirteen She stared at him intently and quickly realised that he was wearing the dark trousers and navy jersey of a sailor. She stared

The Tailor's Daughter ~ 69

at him with eyes wide open and then was joined by her older sisters Fanny, Amy and Minnie.

"My name is Frederick Gosley" he announced. Then just when he thought there couldn't be any more women, little Annie came to the front of the crowd closely followed by her mother and even more sisters.

"Come on girls, get out of the way – I can't see anything for blinkin' skirts!" Finally a male voice and strong arms gently pushed the girls away. "Don't you know this man has just been two months on the high seas, come in my boy, come in."

Thomas Adshead introduced himself and his wife.

Frederick saw a comely bespectacled man with a kindly face covered in whiskers and he was just as Charlotte had described. Her mother, also Charlotte, was bigger built than her daughter and had round rosy cheeks and a cockney accent that you could almost cut with a knife but you could see the likeness to her offspring.

"Come in my boy" she pushed the girls out of the way and Frederick finally saw the face of young Thomas, the only boy in a household of girls.

"I hope you are going to look after my sister!" said the little boy cheekily.

"Thomas!" cried Minnie "give it time, the man hasn't asked father yet!"

Frederick smiled and put his bag down as Mrs Adshead ushered him to the table and poured some soup out in front of him.

"Looks like you all know what I am here for then doesn't it" he laughed.

"Well get on with it then!" said seventeen year old Amy.

"Amy! I despair!" said Minnie.

"Yes, lets have a bit of bloomin' decorum," said Mother.

Frederick turned to the man who he hoped would be his future father-in-law.

"Mr. Adshead, can I have the honour of asking for your daughter's hand in marriage?"

Thomas paused just to tease the girls. Then –

"yes of course my boy, but....."

Nobody heard what the 'but' was as the cheers from all the girls rang around the room.

"Now" said Mrs. Adshead, "you drink your soup and tell us everything about New Zealand and what our daughter is doing."

"And", said Thomas as he decided to get practical again, "later on you can tell me all about how you are going to provide for my girl."

"I get good wages Mr. Adshead, and my father is very comfortably placed, although I don't think it will ever be necessary to require any assistance from him. I'm also hoping to perhaps give up the sea and Charlotte and I can open a lodging house."

Thomas seemed well satisfied. He had taken to Frederick, he seemed like a very level headed young man and he also liked the faint touch of arrogance that he had about him. Eventually the women and young Thomas retired and the two men talked way into the night. Mrs Adshead had made him up a bed in a corner of the Tailors shop and when he settled down for the night, with the sound of the occasional horses hoof on the cobbles outside, he was well satisfied with this part of his mission. He would just have time to pay a visit down to Deal to see his parents before getting back to the ship and preparing it for the journey back to New Zealand.

The following morning he bid farewell to the bevy of beauties that were the Adshead sisters and Charlotte's parents and little brother and hailed down a cab to take him to the train station. Even these had improved since he was last home and he would be down in Kent by the end of the day.

❖ ❖ ❖

It was Jane Gosley that first saw her son coming down the road. He had been absent for well over a year but there was no mistaking the sailor's gate and the purposeful stride as he came towards her. James had learned that the SS British Empire had arrived in English waters so she knew that it would only be a matter of time before Frederick would come home to see them.

She dashed from the window and flung open the door, at the same time calling to her husband.

"James, James! It's Frederick – he's home!"

The pair rushed out of the house and flung their arms around him in a loving embrace while the young servant girl, Emily, looked on from a distance.

"My goodness Frederick" said Jane, "you have filled out my son, the New Zealand life must be doing you good."

"It's good to see you mother" smiled Frederick as he wrapped his arms around her and hugged his father. "I have so much to tell you, and you me, and in such a short space of time."

"Well come on, come on", thundered James, "come on my boy and tell me all about this young lady you are proposing to marry."

Frederick followed his parents into the familiar surroundings of the house in Deal while Emily busied herself in the kitchen preparing tea.

"I may give up the sea father" he eventually said, "I think it is time to move on and there are so many opportunities in New Zealand."

Deep down James didn't blame him. It was a hard life and both he and his father before him had done it all their lives, but that was in the days when there were plenty of jobs for Cinque Port Pilots around the coasts of Britain. These days, with the big ocean going ships, you were away from loved ones for years on end. He remembered piloting the British King around the coast of Kent to pick its passengers up in Plymouth, a job he had done so many times. But the ships were getting bigger and bigger and he certainly would not like to be responsible for one of those great monsters. Jane had other issues on her mind.

"You will come home one day though won't you Frederick," she said. "What with young James being away at sea as we speak and poor Francis up in Scotland, I feel as though I am losing all my sons."

"Now, now wife" chastised James, "that's enough, the children have to make their own way in life," but deep down he echoed his wife's sentiments.

"Oh mother, the distance from the Antipodes to England gets shorter by the day, and just wait until we can go through the Suez Canal and avoid the Cape – then the journey will be shorter by weeks. All I need to do is do well in whatever venture I undertake so that I can afford the journey. Now you tell me all about Frank."

Frederick's young brother was Frank to everyone but his mother who usually called him Francis.

Once again Frederick found himself talking into the night. James had two days holiday from work and so there was plenty to chat about and the men enjoyed each others company, both in the house and at the local Tavern while Jane and Emily made sure they wanted for nothing. It was good to be home but

Frederick could not wait to get back to Charlotte and start a new life in New Zealand.

❖ ❖ ❖

It was the spring of 1886 when Charlotte and Frederick finally married in Holy Trinity Church, Lyttleton.

Frederick enjoyed the break with his parents except for having to try and curb his mother's tears as he said goodbye. He also considered himself fortunate to have met Charlotte's parents and to formally ask for her hand in marriage.

"Goodness me" he had said to Charlotte, "I couldn't believe how many sisters you have. Poor little Thomas looked quite overwhelmed."

Clearly the dashing sailor had been a success with them all because he brought back a letter with him from her father giving his blessing to the marriage.

"Just as well" thought Charlotte, "there wouldn't have been much they could do about it even if they didn't approve of Frederick." However, she was pleased that he had been accepted.

She had not been idle while her fiancé had been on his voyages. She had made her own wedding dress and had already made arrangements with Jenny and James Braithwaite to temporarily rent a small house owned by them. This would become available for them after the marriage and in the meantime Charlotte would remain in her room at the Sailor's Return. Frederick for the time being had his cabin on board the ship whilst it was in dock. However, more plans had to be made and top of the list was to inform the Captain of the SS British Empire that he didn't want to sign on for any more years with ocean going ships and would seek employment with the Wellington Harbour Board. Then, maybe one day he and Charlotte could open their proposed lodging house. It was with mixed feelings that he broke the news to the Captain and then, bit by bit, to the crew. He would miss their comradeship – they had literally been through hell and high water together but he was in his mid thirties now and he saw a different life ahead of him with Charlotte. He waited impatiently to be summoned by the Captain to be told whether he had got his wish.

"I'm so sorry my boy" said Captain Jones kindly, "We will all miss you, but they could do with some good pilots around Wellington. The place is like a madhouse!"

The fast growing city was two hundred miles away and Frederick had got quite used to coming back to the comparative peace and cosiness of Lyttleton. He didn't know what Charlotte would say as he hadn't told her yet. He wanted to check everything out first. It would certainly be preferable to the long trips that took him away for nearly a year. He thanked the Captain and braced himself to impart the news when he got back up to the 'Sailor's Return'.

"Wellington?" said Charlotte and Jenny together..

"I'm afraid so my dear," said Frederick as he sat down in the chair and allowed James to pour him some beer. "That's where the work is."

"Never mind," said Jenny gently, "we shall miss you two, but you have your whole lives before you and..." She turned away and quickly brushed away a tear. "and I am sure we can have plenty of visits."

"Get off with you young man," said James Braithwaite gruffly, "you had better get cracking and get yourself a trip over to North Island and find yourselves some lodgings to go to, otherwise this poor girl will be left on her own again."

In actual fact Charlotte was not too badly disposed towards moving to Wellington. She remembered when her ship had called there and she had enjoyed the brief walk around she'd had. It was a thriving place and slightly reminded her of the hustle and bustle of London and it wouldn't be a bad place to bring up children.

And so it was that Frederick would have to have another trip away, this time on a small inter-island vessel to report to the new place of employment and to secure a home for his wife to be. There was indeed much to be done and drinking beer at the 'Sailor's Return' was not helping the situation.

They were married in the little stone church and Andrew acted as Best Man whilst James Braithwaite gave Charlotte away. The wedding was attended by scores of sailors and people who had got to know the couple over the past two years. She threw her bouquet over her shoulder and it was caught by Harriet who had originally been in her cabin on the British King on that harrowing journey from England. It was a happy day only slightly tinged with sadness because their parents were so far away on the other side of the world and they were going to be moving from this area they had got to know so well. Frederick read her thoughts.

"Don't worry my dear" he whispered, "we will go back one day I am sure and Wellington is not all that far either."

Then, all of a sudden, just as they were coming out of church they noticed a change in the atmosphere. Everywhere went dark and there seemed to be a lot of dust everywhere.

"That's strange!" exclaimed Frederick, "whatever can have caused that?"

"Perhaps there has been an earthquake somewhere," suggested Jenny as she helped Charlotte onto her carriage next to Frederick.

The following day they all found out exactly what it had been and still the strange dust and blackness hung in the air. Mount Tarawera which was right at the top of the North Island near to Auckland had erupted and had killed nearly one hundred and fifty people, mostly Maori. The ash and the debris had travelled as far south as Christchurch. It seemed almost unbelievable.

"Oh those poor people," said Charlotte "whatever must it have been like for us to feel it as far away as this?"

And so the happiness of the wedding ended in a more subdued way than had originally been planned. Nevertheless they had much to look forward to despite the dark cloud that the sun could not penetrate through and the dust falling on their clothes. They all knew that with the prevailing winds the mess would soon clear. That, however, would do nothing to help the poor souls who had been closely affected by this freak of nature.

Despite everything the newly weds were seen off in style and boarded a small ship to take them to their new home in New Zealand's capital city. All Charlotte could do was hope against hope that Frederick had found them somewhere nice.

They both stood on board and waved frantically to the little knot of people who had come to the jetty to see them off. Charlotte was laughing and crying at the same time and filled with anticipation for the future.

❖ ❖ ❖

The newly weds were pleased with the rented house that Frederick had secured. It was in the centre of Wellington in the busy Boulcott Street. It was certainly an area that seemed to be on the move and even had some of the contraptions that she had seen in London driving slowly down the street. Horseless carriages that frightened the animals and made her wonder just what the future had in store. Would everyone travel by these things one day?

Boulcott Street in the 1880s

Wellington was a busy city crammed into a limited space between the sea and the mountains with a temperature not much different to England. It had been established for little more than fifty years but there were many grand buildings and Charlotte marvelled at the architecture as well as the breathtaking scenery. There was the magnificent Government Building which she had seen on her last visit, but also the beautiful Gothic church which they called Old St.Paul's Cathedral, all made with timber and magnificent stained glass windows. It had been build some twenty years ago and designed by the

Reverend Frederick Thatcher who was still the vicar of the parish although very advanced in years.

She had been sorry to leave Lyttleton Harbour and all the people she had got to know but this was a lovely city at the mouth of the harbour and with the glorious mountains in the background. She thought she was on the edge of yet another adventure.

They were not to remain at Boulcott Street for long though. After a short while and with Charlotte becoming pregnant they decided to rent a place in Nelson Street which was just across the bay and nearer to the offices of the Wellington Harbour Board that Fredrick would be working for.

It was at Nelson Street that their first child was born on the 8th February 1886, but sadly the little mite was not long for this world. They had already made up their minds to call the baby James Morehouse after Frederick's father if it were to be a boy. But it was a long labour for Charlotte, and the child was a weak little thing. He finally gave up the struggle for life just a fortnight later on 23rd February. Doctor Kemp wrote out the death certificate and put the cause down as exhaustion.

Charlotte was devastated.

"How? Why? Where did I go wrong?" she cried.

"You did nothing wrong lass" replied the kindly Doctor. "It's just one of those things. He just gave up the struggle for life poor little chap."

"We shall have more children," muttered Frederick awkwardly.

But Charlotte could not be consoled. She hadn't even told her parents she was pregnant yet! Now she felt terrible at keeping it from them. It had been months before she had even realised that she was with child. With everything that had been happening she had failed to notice that her body was not working each month as it should do. Only her ever expanding waistline caused her to mention something to Jenny.

"Why, you are clearly pregnant, you silly girl," Jenny had chided her.

In fact it had turned out that she was already six months pregnant and with Frederick away at sea she did not want to write home to her parents until she had been able to tell him. By the time Frederick was home, and he could see for himself, it was all too late.

"I'll write to them once the baby has arrived," she said. "I want to see if it is a boy and then it will be a nice surprise to write about after all those girls in the family."

Now the baby was dead from exhaustion and it was all too much to bear. Charlotte was totally dismayed and continued to blame herself.

"Perhaps it is because I am nearly thirty!" she exclaimed, "maybe the good Lord does not want me to have babies."

"Nonsense!" said Jenny when she came on one of her frequent visits. "Why, it is so very common to lose babies within a few days. I have lost four and then I couldn't have anymore after that."

Of course, when Charlotte thought about it rationally she did realise that Jenny was making sense. She did know, of course, that she had lost some babies but not four, and of course, her own mother had lost two. Even so, she could still not get the feeling of guilt out of her mind, more because she had not even told her parents that she was pregnant anyway. How could she write to them now and say that they had a grandson and lost it all in the space of two weeks!

They laid the child to rest in the Cemetery of the Church where they were married just a year before and Charlotte, with her usual gritty determination, put the matter behind her and made her mind up that she would start to make the best of their new home in Nelson Street and look to the future. She decided to let sleeping dogs lie as far as the folks back home in England were concerned. What they didn't know would not hurt them.

"What's the point Frederick!" she said to her husband one day when they took some flowers to the little grave. "They never need know – both our parents are old and it is not fair to make them sad."

Frederick wasn't too happy about not telling them, but he could see her point. He didn't fancy the idea of telling his father James Morehouse that his namesake had only been alive for a fortnight, especially on top of learning about Francis and his blindness. Instead they decided to just keep baby James in their hearts and hope that the next child will be healthier.

Charlotte soon got to know her neighbours. One in particular was Flora from next door and, who as her name suggested, came from Scotland. She had come to New Zealand on the SS Aurora, which was the first immigrant ship, back in the 1830s as a new bride.

She was now in her seventies and widowed. Even though she had been away from Scotland all that time she still retained her accent, had seen it all and knew everybody. She was a short stocky little woman with steely grey hair all pushed up on top of her head in a bun.

"Och, you just come in for a wee bevy" she had said when they first arrived. "Come away in and you tell old Flora if you need anything."

She liked the woman and she was certainly a pleasure to be with and take advantage of her vast knowledge of the surrounding area, even to the point of telling her which was the best butcher or baker in the area or the history of the Government buildings.

"Och, it's the Governor General who stays there hen, his name is Sir William Francis Drummond Jervois." She giggled, "now there's a mouthful for you."

Yes, she was getting used to the place but it was now just a question of saving some money so that they could rent a larger establishment and start their lodging house. Then her husband would be home permanently.

It wasn't long before she found herself to be pregnant again and on 22nd February 1887 their little girl was born. Keeping with family tradition they called her Charlotte Jane after the two grandmothers.

At first they were too terrified to leave the baby for even a minute, taking turns in watching her every move but as the weeks went by they felt more confident and they were able to write home and tell the families about the arrival of little Charlotte.

"All these Charlottes" laughed Frederick after yet another night of lost sleep, "it's so confusing, what with your Mother, and you and now this little one. She may be Charlotte to you my darling but she will have to be Lottie to me."

She was a beautiful baby with a mop of dark hair and she became the main attraction among the neighbours..

"Oh its wonderful to have a baby around" cooed Flora whose children had long since left home. "she is so bonny and so good."

Charlotte was soon able to take Lottie for walks in the countryside which wasn't that far away from the town, or sometimes a stroll down to the dockside to wait to see Frederick's ship arrive back whenever he went away. That is, of course, when he did come home! Even though he was on the shorter routes around the North and South Islands of New Zealand, sometimes he was still away a week at a time. However, if the couple thought that their troubles were now over they were to be sadly mistaken! In fact their lives were about to be changed for ever.

❖ ❖ ❖

7.   A Change in Circumstances

It was towards the end of the year as the New Zealand summer heralded the start of winter back home in England, that Frederick first got a clue that something was wrong. Charlotte was busying herself in the kitchen making pastry. He had little Lottie on his knee and with his spare hand he was turning over the pages of the newspaper catching up on the news and finding out more about the awful volcano eruption that had happened on their wedding day. Two years on and they were still finding bodies. Suddenly, to his horror, he found he couldn't read it. He leaped to his feet and put the child down on the floor.

"Charlotte!" he called, "Charlotte darling, can you read the print in this paper?"

She came running into the room and looked to where he was pointing.

"Why yes Frederick, of course I can!" she cried "what is the matter with you?"

Frederick didn't dare relay to Charlotte the fear that had suddenly gripped him by the throat.

"Oh maybe I just need spectacles" he laughed a little unconvincingly. "I'll go into Wellington tomorrow and see the doctor."

"I shall come with you," said Charlotte.

"No, no need!" he retorted quickly, "I'll get a carriage. You stay and look after Lottie." Surely history could not be repeating itself – could it?

Charlotte seemed satisfied and Frederick tried to convince himself that it was just because he needed spectacles – after all he was in his mid thirties now. He gulped – but surely thirty-five wasn't that old really. He went to bed that night hoping against hope that there would be an improvement by morning in his ability to read the paper.

There wasn't. Even in the bright daylight of the early morning, everything looked blurred and Frederick suddenly felt a surge of panic. What on earth would be the use of a ship's navigator who couldn't see properly? He tried trimming his beard and found himself squinting into the mirror like an old man.

"I *am* coming with you!" Charlotte insisted again, "no arguments now Frederick – I'll get Lottie ready. It isn't far."

Suddenly her husband seemed to have all the arrogance and stuffing knocked out of him and his wife feared what this turn of events might mean. She hadn't forgotten his stories about his brother and neither had he. Suddenly she knew she had to take charge of things.

"Wait there Frederick!" she said, trying very hard to hold back her tears as she got the baby ready, "wait there and I'll be back in just a minute. I'll go and tell Flora and then we can go."

"Why what on earth is the matter hen?" she gasped as she opened the door and saw how flustered Charlotte was.

"I'm not sure yet" said Charlotte, "but it is my belief that Frederick is losing his sight."

"Oh my dear, my dear, lets hope you are wrong," cried Flora. "Maybe it is just that he needs some good spectacles hen. Nevertheless, you run along now and don't you worry about a thing.

Within ten minutes she was back indoors and it took all of her will power to avoid crying and make light of the matter as she concentrated on putting Lottie in the pram.

The Tailor's Daughter ~ 85

"Flora says it could be that you need spectacles" she tried to reassure him. "They can do such wonderful things with spectacles these days – my father wears them all the time."

"Whoever heard of a sailor with spectacles, and a navigator at that!" snapped Frederick, and then immediately gave Charlotte a hug as he realised that it was not her fault and that she was just trying her best. He tried to look at the imposing new buildings as they trundled along the road with the pram past Government House. Charlotte described them to him.

"Oh Frederick, see how big it is and with its bright red roof."

He could make out the shape but it was very blurred and he could not see the hills in the distance at all even though he knew they were there. They looked fuzzy and blurred and he certainly could not see the sheep that he knew covered them. He knew definitely that his eyesight was certainly not as it should be. He glanced sideways at Charlotte's face and realised with a shock that he could barely make out her features. He felt it was the longest walk of his life and it was with very mixed feelings that he strode into the Doctor's waiting room, his mind filled with anticipation as to what might be said to him. Unless there was a miracle cure he could not go back to work.

They made their way into the room and braced themselves for what was to come. The torture was made even worse because they had to wait behind a queue of people with various ailments all seated on the chairs in a row and Lottie chose that very moment to start crying for food. A nurse came and led Charlotte to a side room where she could feed the baby, though she wasn't sure which was worse, seeing the Doctor or the waiting, but at least feeding Lottie passed the time.

Eventually though, Frederick's name was called and Charlotte waited patiently while he disappeared into the surgery of

Doctor Thomas Williams. She sat staring at the closed door as if she could detect what was going on through the white painted woodwork. After what seemed like an eternity the doctor came to the door and beckoned to her.

"I think you are needed with your husband my dear."

She followed him meekly and thankfully the baby slept in her arms. She was greeted by the sight of Frederick sitting by the table with his head in his hands and looking quite ashen.

"I don't think we can do anything for him here" said Doctor Williams. "I've seen this before and I think he could be going blind, especially in view of the fact that it has already happened to his younger brother. It looks like Glaucoma to me."

Charlotte felt faint and grabbed hold of the side of the desk as the doctor pushed a chair behind her.

"Its true my dear" said Frederick, "the worst is happening of that I am sure."

"I am in no position to say for definite," went on Doctor Williams, "I don't have the equipment and I may be wrong. You need a second opinion and you need the advice and treatment by experts, none of which is available in New Zealand."

Both Charlotte and Frederick felt as though their world was caving in. All their plans were going to come to nothing.

What on earth was going to happen to them? She heard the voice of the doctor as if it was speaking to someone else. This couldn't be happening – could it? She tried to concentrate on what the doctor was saying and sat down on the nearest chair.

"The best advice I can give you," he went on, "is to go back to England and go to The Moorfields Eye Hospital. They are the experts and if they can not help you then no one can."

"That's where my brother went," said Frederick glumly, "and they were not able to cure him."

Suddenly Charlotte summoned up all the courage she could muster and took charge of the situation. If there was some hope left and it lay back in London they would go back.

"Then that is what we will do," she said, "we will go home – neither of our families are poor and I am sure they will help us." She had made up her mind. "Frederick, we will go home as soon as we can get a passage and who knows, maybe one day we will still be able to have that little guest house we had planned."

Frederick could not see the tears that were falling down her face but he could see enough and, as yet, he wasn't totally blind. Maybe this was as bad as it was going to get.

They finally took their leave of the Doctor and made their way out into the street. As they pushed the pram down the hill they walked in silence, each lost in their own thoughts.

Frederick was thinking about his job on the shorter haul routes from Wellington to Hawke's Bay. He missed the comradeship of the lads on the 'British Empire', especially Andrew but it had been two years now and he had settled into his position working for the Wellington Harbour Board. It was a position which was far more suitable for a man with a wife and child than going away for six months at a time on an Immigration ship.

His friend had been beside himself at the very idea of losing Frederick to another ship but understood the situation. One thing was for sure, his time working on any sort of ship was well and truly over now.

Charlotte was thinking about making the trip home with a baby and what sort of a journey it would be. It was bad enough when she only had herself to think about so gawd knows what it would be like now. Would James Gosley or Thomas Adshead help them out until they could become established, and, most important of all, was her husband really going to be blind? Many, many questions – the answers were yet to come. Moreover, if Frederick had harboured any doubts about keeping the death of little James from his parents before, those doubts disappeared with this latest blow. Both his sons going blind was enough for the old couple to cope with. The baby was born in New Zealand and died in New Zealand and thats where the secret would remain.

As soon as Charlotte went to tell Flora she was back from the Doctors the old lady could see something was amiss. The younger woman could hold her tears back no longer and wept in her arms.

"Dinna fret hen," said Flora, "I am sure things will work oot for you – they can do so much today and anytime you need me to help you out or to look after Lottie you just say so." She held Charlotte's arm, "you just say so hen."

"Remember lassie," went on Flora, "you must be the strong one in the family and don't let Frederick see how upset you are it will only make matters worse."

And so it was that when she went indoors she pulled herself together and was ready to face whatever fate had in store. She found Frederick sitting in the chair trying desperately to read the paper by holding it close to his face and Lottie in the crib at his side.

"Don't worry husband!" she said gently, "we will sort this out and I will be beside you all the way."

He kissed her cheek and stroked her hair. What would he do without her? He had come all the way to New Zealand to find her and she was the best thing that had ever happened to him.

The fact remained though that he would soon be out of work. He had a small pension from the shipping company but it would not be enough to live on for long. They would have to go home and he would have to figure out a way to earn a living. It was with some relief when he heard from his sailor friends, some who frequented the Sailor's Return at Lyttleton that the SS British Empire was calling into the Harbour and then coming on to Wellington and carrying mostly cargo. At least Charlotte would be able to write a letter home, and with a bit of luck it would be there before them so that the family were prepared for what was to come. In the meantime he would have to try and secure a passage on the next ship after that and then telegraph his parents. At least that was one good thing. The telegraph system had come into general use and, at a cost, you could send a message to anywhere in the world. The world was getting smaller by the minute. But still they had not told their parents about the death of little James.

Despite the fact that she had a child to contend with it was Charlotte that took control. She wrote a letter home and she also wrote to the shipping company on behalf of Frederick pleading their case and asking for a passage home on the next ship due to go to England. She was not looking forward to the journey one little bit but it had to be done. She also wrote to Jenny Braithwaite and as soon as she heard the news she wrote a long comforting letter back and that helped.

It was nice to know that people back at Lyttleton were thinking of them. All she wanted now though was to get home to England and hope and pray that The Moorfields Eye Hospital in London would be able to work its magic. If they just were able to stop it getting any worse it would be something. All this took priority over any plans she had previously made to make a new life for herself in New Zealand and she put her disappointment to one side.

What neither Charlotte nor Frederick bargained for was that the influx of immigrants from England to New Zealand was slowing down and there were fewer big ships during 1887. They were also waiting to hear from the Shipping Company as to whether they had a passage home. It was a lot to ask. They had the money for one fare but not enough for two and a child. To get the money from home would take longer than the wait for a ship. All they could do was to rely on the good offices of the Company and of Frederick's reputation as a good First Mate for all those years. She also offered her services as a ships cook.

They tried to spend as much time as they could going around the Wellington area and taking in the breathtaking views, knowing that for both of them it would all soon be over.

It was magical to see the blossom on the trees and feel the warmth of the sunshine against ones face as Christmas approached and also still odd to think that here the festive season was in the summertime.

They made the best of the time among the friends they had made at their new home. They had turkey and mince pies whilst watching Lottie try to toddle and fall down with a thump on her backside after a few steps. It was almost possible to forget the traumas of the past months and to pretend that all of this would come to an end, especially as Frederick's eyesight seemed to stabilise for a while. Only the thought of seeing the family again sweetened the bitter pill of having to give up all their plans. Also, of course, baby Charlotte was a New Zealand citizen by birthright. Who knows, maybe she would be back one day.

❖ ❖ ❖

The weather was starting to turn cold again and it was early in 1888 when finally they heard from the shipping company that they could have free passages on the SS British King and that Charlotte could help out in the galley. It was the very ship that Charlotte had gone to New Zealand in four years ago captained by Captain Kelly. Was it really just four years? It seemed like an eternity in one way and yet it had gone so quickly. The last few weeks had not gone quickly for Frederick though. He did not like being unemployed and only his daughter and helping with the packing and the disposal of their goods kept him from going insane. Fortunately most of their furniture had come with the rented house, but there was still plenty of luggage to pack and also sell. Every penny would help towards the trip home.

It was hard to pack the trunk and say goodbye to everyone and Charlotte refused to leave without seeing the Braithwaites. She wrote to Jenny to say that they would look out for her when their ship called in at Lyttleton Harbour. It would be its last port of call before heading for the open sea and the arduous journey back to Britain.

It was extremely difficult to say goodbye to Flora.

"Don't you worry hen", she said as she gave Charlotte a massive hug and clutched her to her ample bosom. "I'm sure we will see each other again, if not in this life then the next, and we can always write to each other, and who knows my dear, maybe one day you…" and then she indicated to the baby, "or Lottie, may come back."

Frederick felt very emotional both with the upset of leaving and with the anticipation of what was in store. His eyesight had not worsened but it was certainly not getting any better either and he could barely see his hand in front of his face. He even had to rely on Charlotte's help to trim his whiskers. If that wasn't bad enough, he also, much to his disgust found that he had no choice but to use a white stick.

"It's not just for you," said Charlotte when he slung it in a temper across the room. "It's to let other people know that you can not see so well. It's not fair to expect everyone to know you can not see and, good gawd Frederick, you don't want carriages running you over."

He did see the sense of it and apologised to his wife for being so grumpy. Now it was part of him and he had it hanging from one arm as they got ready to board the ship and their luggage was stowed away.

She felt strangely confident. It would take a couple of days to get to Lyttleton and then they could settle down properly to the main voyage once they got there and said a few more goodbyes. Also they would telegraph a message home.

Charlotte put Lottie in the pram. She had remembered from her trip out how some mothers had their prams with them. They were cumbersome to store but ideal for taking the children around the ship on the long voyage.

She didn't know what to expect. The journey out to New Zealand had been awful enough, but now she had more than herself just to think about.

There were more hugs and more tears with Flora and some of the other neighbours until, finally, the little family went up the familiar gangplank to the promenade deck of the SS British King. Charlotte shivered as a feeling of de-ja-vu sweep over her when she pushed the pram onto the deck. She held onto the rail and saw old Flora standing by the quayside waving.

"Oh Frederick, hold the pram – I must wave." He held onto the pram with one hand and with the other he waved to a crowd of people that he could not see.

The Tailor's Daughter

They both knew it would be a little while before the ship got underway so it was time to make their way to their cabin which was in second class. Now they could lift Lottie from the pram and allow it to be put into the storage compartment on the Promenade deck. She knew the way but she allowed a swarthy looking seaman to escort them and show them to the cabin that the shipping company had reserved for them.

She was pleased also to see that their trunk had already arrived and all that remained was to settle themselves in. It was slightly different to the cabin she had shared with the girls on the way out from England. This one had a double bed and a cot and really wasn't too bad. She found herself wondering what the first class cabins looked like and thought they must be very posh indeed.

Then came the unmistakable sound of the ship's engines starting up and the whole place seemed to judder.

"Will you be all right here?" she said to her husband. She put the baby in one of the cots. "You keep an eye on her for I would really like to see the ship leave and I must see if I can be of use in the galley."

"Yes, off you go darling," replied Frederick. "There is not much I will be able to see anyway."

She felt so sorry for him and leaned over and gave him a kiss.

"I'll not be long, I promise."

She made her way up the steps to the promenade deck just as the ship was pulling away from the jetty and the chains that had been holding it steady fell away and dropped into the water. Now there was a huge crowd of people all seeing the ship off on its way but she could still make out the unmistakable figure of Flora and some of the neighbours that she had got to know. She waved back while the tears coursed unchecked down her cheeks.

She pulled her coat further around her shoulders against the chill of the wind and there was a few flakes of snow in the air as the vessel moved down the inlet and she saw the tiny figures on the quayside turn into little dots in the distance and then finally disappear as the huge vessel cruised out into the open sea. Finally she made her way to the galley to see if there was anything she could do. Indeed there was. Within no time Frederick was in charge of little Lottie and she was ready to start work helping out the Ship's Cook.

❖ ❖ ❖

8. The Journey Home

Frederick was happy enough looking after Lottie but Charlotte still needed to be a mother some of the time and feed her child. There were two different arrangements for feeding older children. Mothers did have the facility to cook their own meals sharing the galley between about six different families, or they could go to the main restaurant where they would be served by the crew. She still had to fulfil her duties in helping out the Cook so looking after Lottie had to fit in with her job. She knew that she would have to take turns between helping in the Galley and then coming back to the cabin to feed Lottie in private. At the same time she did not want to leave Frederick on his own for too long.

She was just debating with herself what was best to do when there was a loud knock on the door.

"Who on earth is that?" said Frederick.

"Come on Freddy old chap, open up and let the dog see the rabbit," said the voice on the other side of the door.

He knew exactly who it was. Frederick would know that voice anywhere.

"It's Andrew!" He rushed to the door as Charlotte hastily did up her dress again.

"Andrew! What brings you here?" he cried, "though I am so glad to see you old boy."

"Got a transfer between ships" said his old friend. "Couldn't let your family travel all that way without someone to keep an eye on you."

Charlotte was delighted. It was the first time she had seen her husband with a smile on his face for ages and she was also very relieved. Now she had a bit of support on the journey although she did appreciate that Andrew was actually there to work, as she was!

"Come on Frederick, lets go and eat, and leave the ladies to themselves." He and Charlotte exchanged smiles as he needed no second asking. Andrew slapped Frederick on the back and the two of them disappeared through the door.

"Don't worry, I'll have him back to you in less than an hour," called Andrew, "I have to be on duty then. Somebody has got to steer the thing."

"And someone has to help with the cooking, so don't you two be too long and get me into trouble," she laughed.

"Well, there is one thing," said Frederick philosophically, as the door shut behind them, "I always said I could find my way blindfolded around the SS British Empire, now I can try it in reality around the British King."

Charlotte wiped a tear from her eye as the two men left but she was glad of the peace to feed the baby and to sort out the luggage. There were laundry facilities on board but experience told her last time that it was best to make do as much as possible. She had plenty of rags and tie-ups with her to keep Lottie from wetting or soiling the bedding. The main thing was to wrap up warm. She shivered – even in the cabin it was chilly and it was getting colder the further the ship got away from New Zealand and out into the open sea. She also knew she had a pile of potatoes to peel in the galley so she hoped that Frederick and Andrew would not be too long.

They were gone long enough for her to feed and wind Lottie in peace and sort the cabin out. Suddenly there was a knock on the door and Frederick arrived having said his goodbyes to Andrew. He was like a different man.

"Come on Charlotte dear, I feel more confident now and Andrew and I have eaten well. It's your turn and the ship's restaurant is not too far away. I'll look after Lottie while you eat."

"I won't be doing too much eating husband," she laughed. "I'm supposed to be helping Cook, remember?" She wasn't all that hungry anyway and very conscious that she had a job of work to do.

They arrived at Lyttleton Harbour in the early hours of the morning and everyone went up on deck to see the ship glide into the bay and slowly make its way to the familiar quayside. Charlotte could make out the hills and the rows of houses in the distance and she was filled with impatience to get ashore and see Jenny and James again. She knew they would have a few hours and it would be good to catch up with everyone and show off the baby to her old friends. She had already got the pram from the storage area.

Then as the ship got nearer she saw the unmistakable sight of Jenny Braithwaite's portly figure waiting for her on the quayside and waving frantically. It seemed like an eternity but finally, with an almighty clunk, the enormous vessel docked and the gangplanks were lowered.

Frederick knew exactly where he was going. He could have disembarked with or without sight, but he hung back and held on to the side of the pram and put his white stick where others could see it. Fortunately he could not see the looks of pity coming in his direction from acquaintances who knew him when he was First Mate on the British Empire and used to come ashore regularly to go to the Sailor's Return.

"Jenny, Jenny, Jenny" Charlotte squealed as she rushed into her friend's arms who clutched her to her ample bosom.

"Oh, let me see this lovely little girl." Jenny was torn between delight and sadness. There had been such tragedy already in their lives with the death of a baby and the loss of Frederick's sight. She felt her eyes welling up as she welcomed the little family ashore.

"Don't you worry my boy," she smiled gently, "you have a good woman to look after you. Best cook the 'Sailor's Return has ever had. Come on, I've left James looking after the beer for you."

"That's what I like to hear," he replied as he put his arm around her shoulders.

Frederick felt a little bit incongruous embarking from the ship in his ordinary clothes and not in his merchant navy uniform but he brushed down his jacket and gave a reassuring tug to his cravat and tried to assume the cocky demeanour that they had always been used to as they trudged up the slope to the familiar surroundings of the hostelry. James Braithwaite was waiting at the door, along with a few faces that Charlotte and Frederick knew only too well – the regulars that frequented the bar almost on a daily basis.

"Come on my girl," twittered Jenny, "bring the child into the back room and you can feed her and see to her needs. Let's leave these men to men's talk."

Charlotte meekly pushed the pram into the back room. It was just as well because Lottie was starting to make herself heard. She was way overdue for a good feed and needed changing.

The two women chattered and looked after the baby and the time sped by all too quickly. Much of the talk was about the misfortune that had befallen Frederick but both agreed that if there was any chance with the Eye Hospital in London then it should be taken.

"You know his brother went blind too?" said Charlotte.

"Yes," replied Jenny, "I met him once when he came here with Frederick, a lovely boy, such a shame."

"We must get back," said Charlotte as she felt the tears well up again, "I'll make the little one clean and see if I can rescue that husband of mine or we shall have that ship going without us."

"I do hope they can do something for him," said Jenny a little unconvincingly, "what a blow to have this thing happen to two brothers."

"I know, I do wonder sometimes if they have upset the good Lord at some time or other," replied Charlotte.

The women went back into the front of the house and found the men deep in conversation and more than one pint of ale had passed their lips. Both were a little louder than they normally would have been.

"Hey ho!" boomed James, "here's the lady wife come to keep an eye on you Freddy old man."

Frederick got up a little unsteadily and put on his jacket. He wasn't too drunk not to realise that they had a ship to board and an extremely long voyage ahead. His wife also had her own duties to attend to although, in truth, she wasn't working anywhere near the hours that the regular cook would work. Basically the company were doing Frederick a favour in allowing her to work her passage.

"I'll lock the place up," said James, "and I'll come and help you to send that telegraph home to England. It will be there before you and then the family will be ready for you."

Charlotte was secretly hoping that her letter would get there but it would certainly be good to send a telegram to be on the safe side. Maybe her father would come and meet them at the Albert Docks. They had already decided that they would disembark in London rather than Plymouth so that Frederick could be on the spot to go to Moorfields which was only just around the corner from her father's tailoring establishment.

The little party made their way down the hill and they could see the ship moored along with others in the harbour. It was a majestic sight. Once again Charlotte felt the tears pricking at the back of her eyes. She knew it would be the last time she would be walking down this hill. She didn't really think they would be back, not now she had a child and another future to plan with a blind husband.

She stood with Jenny at the quayside and waited until the men appeared after sending the telegram. She didn't have a clue how this new fangled system worked. There seemed to be so many new things and she couldn't keep up with it all. How you could possibly telegraph a message from the other side of the world and it get to its destination almost instantly was totally beyond her comprehension. As they were both a little the worse for drink she could only hope that the message made sense.

They heard the change in tone of the ship's engines and some of the crew appeared to raise the gangplanks. It was time to go. Again there were hugs and kisses and promises. James slapped Frederick on the back.

"You will be fine old boy," he boomed "you can't keep an old salt down."

Charlotte and Jenny gave each other one last hug and Jenny kissed Lottie.

The Tailor's Daughter

"Good luck my little one and safe journey," she said. She held Charlotte's hand in both of hers.

"You have still time to have many more children my dear," she smiled. "I'm sure there will be a new little brother or sister for Lottie before long."

Once again the tears flowed as Charlotte pushed the pram up to the promenade deck and waited for Frederick. Crowds of passengers were leaning over the ship's rail trying to catch the minute that the vessel started to pull away. There was a judder and then a foot of clear water appeared between the side of the ship and the jetty, then two feet, then three.....

"Goodbye, goodbye!!" they all shouted.

Charlotte could see Jenny and James waving as if their arms would fall off among the rest of the crowd at the quayside. Frederick could see vague shapes but waved anyway. Suddenly he turned towards her.

"Oh Charlotte dear, I am so sorry that I had to be the cause of this upset – maybe you should have let me come on my own and you stay with Jenny and have your adventures."

"Don't talk silly Frederick!" she snapped "I have had four years of adventure, and, who knows, there may be another one waiting for us around the corner."

They stood on the promenade deck despite the cold wind and waved until the ship turned out of the bay and into the open sea. The child was warm and tucked up in the pram but it was a bitter wind and Charlotte was already turning her thoughts towards warmer weather.

They made their way down to their cabin and settled Lottie into bed. She had been very well fed at Jenny's so there was no need to worry about eating just yet.

"I think I'll use the galley when we do need to eat" said Charlotte, "that way we can eat altogether. Also I can be of more use helping out if needed.

There was a knock on the door and Andrew appeared.

"Just got five minutes peace now we are out to sea" he said, "just thought I'd let you know that they forecast a gale."

"Oh thank you for nothing Andrew" said Charlotte "in that case I'll try and avoid cooking – maybe I should let the expert ship's cooks do it and I'll do the washing up."

He chuckled, "might as well eat before the ship gets too far out to sea or you will be throwing it up.

"Gawd!" thought Charlotte, "What have I let myself in for."

Lyttleton Harbour 1880s

Andrew had been right about the forthcoming gale. For four whole days and nights most passengers stayed in their cabins as the ship tossed and turned in the most horrendous of snow and hail storms and terrific winds. For Charlotte it certainly was not funny trying to feed a baby with a ship tossing from side to side and alternating it with helping in the kitchens, and feeling sick. However, Lottie seemed to take it all in her stride and was totally unaffected by the continuous heaving motion of three and a half thousand tons of ship.

Up in the restaurant any attempt to eat was interrupted by various people either falling on the floor or their plates sliding across the table and the contents ending up in a heap on the deck. Only Frederick seemed unaffected. It was home from home to him and Charlotte marvelled at his ability to find his way around and not be ill or in any way laid low by the continual rocking of the vessel. The sails had long since been furled up and the engines came into their own as the SS British King made its way across the Ocean heading north west. At one point Charlotte did venture up onto the promenade deck and there was nothing to be seen but sea in every direction and huge waves that enveloped the whole ship. She felt the sturdy arm of one of the sailors grab her and she soon went back below decks and continued with the washing up. She decided that caution was the better part of valour!

She wished she had the constitution of the rest of her family. Lottie was sweetly oblivious to the whole adventure and Frederick treated it as if nothing was happening untoward!

Eventually though, the gale did blow itself out and as the ship started to move away from the Antarctic climes so the weather got calmer and warmer and it was quite pleasant. After a week of sailing, she was able to fetch the pram out of storage and use it to perambulate Lottie around the deck. It gave her time to meet some of the other families who were going back home.

In the cabin next door to them there was Rose and her two children. She quickly befriended them and learned that poor Rose had become a widow soon after arriving in New Zealand.

"I suppose you can call me a quitter" she said to Charlotte ruefully, "but I didn't want to bring them up on my own, not when I have family back home in England. I love New Zealand but I decided to go back home to Surrey which is where I come from."

She was a pretty girl with lovely blonde hair done up in a roll around her head like her own but she was slim and beautiful and much too young to have been left so cruelly on her own.

Charlotte thought it was so very sad and it put things in perspective for her. She thought her world was coming to an end when she learned that Frederick was losing his sight, but at least she still had him with her. She did not know what she would have done if left with just the child. The two women made good company for each other and occasionally Charlotte was able to leave Lottie with Frederick and spend time with Rose thus making the journey infinitely more pleasant, or sometimes the two women would walk around the deck pushing the children in their prams. It could have been a day out in the park but for the swell of the sea and the distinct lack of anything, anywhere on any horizon.

Over time the little Gosley family settled into a routine and, together with the occasional visit from Andrew to keep Frederick company and Charlotte's time spent with Rose, and her work in the kitchens, the days seemed to drift by reasonably quickly.

Perhaps it was having a child and a nearly blind husband to look after, or perhaps it was all those potatoes she had to peel, but the journey was certainly going quicker than the original trip to New Zealand and before she knew it a week had gone by, then another week and then another, until finally, in tropical

The Tailor's Daughter ~ 105

heat, they arrived at Cape Town and took on more stores and fuel.

This time she decided not to go ashore. It was not seemly for a married lady with a child to go off accompanied by strange men and she certainly did not intend going alone. She was content to stay on board in the sunshine and watch all the activity of people coming and going and the antics of the natives as they tried to get the passengers to buy their wares.

The loading up of the stores all seemed to go smoothly and the ships crew were happy enough until the order and routine was suddenly interrupted by an uproar.

"Whatever is going on?" said Frederick and stared unseeingly in the direction of the commotion.

"One of the passengers has tried to bring a monkey on board" replied one of the crew in answer. "Silly devil – now the thing has escaped and we have to catch it."

Rose and Charlotte roared with laughter as everyone, it seemed, all tried to catch the monkey. One of the younger toffs from First Class tried to smuggle it on board under his coat but it had quite suddenly given him a bite and he dropped it. Now it was up the main mast and swinging as if it was in the wild from rope to rope.

Just as one sailor got within a tail's width of him so the monkey shot off in another direction, while from the Bridge of the vessel the Ship's Captain and First Mate watched in awe at the ensuing chaos.

Eventually though, the animal was caught – nobody quite knew by whom – and it was duly left in its own country as the crew busied themselves with the job in hand, that of lifting the anchor and setting off again while Charlotte hurried off to do her duties in the galley. It was a bit of light relief and it was talked about over supper for days.

The heat was unbearable as they crossed the equator and so once again, they stayed below decks in the comparative cool. Now, instead of trying to keep Lottie warm, Charlotte had to keep her from overheating and, more to the point, keep her from getting any form of disease. Word had spread round the ship that one child had been isolated because of measles and so she was even more determined to keep her from mixing with other children. When word reached her that the child with the measles had died that 'put the tin hat on it'. She opted to cook the meals for the family in the galley and keep Lottie away from the restaurant all together. She was minded of the child who had died on the journey out to New Zealand, not long before reaching Auckland – she did not intend it to be 'three in a row'.

The little mite was buried at sea and the ship's doctor eventually gave the 'all clear' because everywhere had been scrubbed and disinfected with carbolic and so gradually people with children ventured back up onto the promenade deck to get some much needed sea air.

It would be autumn in England when they arrived home so of course it would gradually get cooler. Like Frederick she wished that the Suez Canal had been opened and then the journey would have been much shorter.

"Oh, one day" said Andrew when he was paying them a quick visit below decks, "one day, the journey will be done in a couple of weeks. You wait and see."

"There are times" replied Charlotte "that I wish I was a bird and I could fly up in the sky and be where I want to be in no time."

"You would have some very painful wings if you were flapping them all the way to New Zealand" laughed Andrew.

"I think it will be possible one day," said Charlotte prophetically, "I read somewhere that some man has invented a thing with wings like a kite that can fly unaided in the sky."

The conversation ended amid peals of laughter and Charlotte went to see if the ship's cooks needed her help.

It was on the last stage of their journey that some terrible news arrived in the form of a signal from a passing ship to the Captain of the 'British King'. Charlotte wondered where the 'passing ship' was, as nothing could be seen on the horizon but Frederick assured her that it was there, out of sight but within an easy distance to send a message. A message that this ship, 'The Crusader" had received from Cape Town who, in turn, had received it from Wellington in New Zealand. There had been a terrific earthquake in the Canterbury area causing much damage to the structures in Christchurch and Lyttleton.

"My God!" exclaimed Frederick when he heard the news "that could have been us!"

There was very little information but gradually it emerged that there had, indeed been a massive earthquake and miraculously no-one had been killed. There was, however, an enormous amount of damage to properties and the spire on the great Cathedral in Christchurch had come crashing to the ground.

All they could do was wonder about the Braithwaites and their friends. Perhaps their homes had been destroyed, perhaps the Sailors Return had suffered. Nobody knew.

"I expect we will find out in the fullness of time" said Charlotte, "I shall write to Jenny as soon as we get home."

"Lets hope she gets it" said Frederick pessimistically, "well, just for once I can say my loss of eyesight did me a favour. We might have been there ourselves – I wouldn't have given that wooden house we lived in much chance in the teeth of an earthquake.

Charlotte was starting to be secretly glad that her New Zealand adventure was all but over.

"Good gawd" she thought to herself, "first a volcano erupts one end of the country and now an earthquake at the other."

After another week at sea there was the familiar sound of seagulls following the ship and they knew that land was not far away. Soon they would be entering the Channel and a succession of pilot ships would guide them around the Kent coast to the mouth of the River Thames and the familiar Albert Dock. She just hoped that the respective families had received her letters and she could only wait for things to unfold.

She washed the same pieces of cloth for napkins for the umpteenth time and took them up on deck to dry in the wind whilst Frederick baby-sat. Suddenly she saw other vessels and the shipping routes were getting busier and busier. She was certainly beginning to understand the need for a pilot ship for guidance. Charlotte was standing looking into the distance as Andrew came along by the side of her.

"Not long now" he said "In a minute you will see the Devon coast and we are heading straight for Plymouth sound. Most of the passengers will be disembarking there but you, of course, will go round to London." He paused for a minute and put his arm round her.

"You are doing a wonderful job you know Charlotte – you will be all right, I know you will."

The Tailor's Daughter ~ 109

Charlotte felt a lump come into her throat and fought hard to keep back the tears. This too was where she would be saying goodbye to Rose and her little family.

"Have you got people to meet you" said Andrew.

"I bloomin' well hope so" she replied, "or my Father is in trouble."

Then he put his hand up to shield his eyes and peered into the distance.

"There look!" he cried "look Charlotte, see that grey patch on the horizon. That's land my girl. We will all soon be home."

She wanted to go rushing to the cabin to tell Frederick but it would be a waste of time. He couldn't see it and he had seen it all before anyway.

"I'd better go" said Andrew "or I will have the Captain after my tail."

She couldn't help wishing that one day Andrew would find himself a good woman. She knew he had several lady friends – a girl in every port as they say – but nobody to settle down with. She was sure that one day he would though as he was such a nice man and she did know that he was sweet on her friend Harriet.

The napkins had all but dried while they had been talking but Charlotte waited for a little longer and gradually as news travelled others came on deck to see the sights of the other ships and the land getting ever closer. She grabbed the napkins and made her way back down to the cabin. Frederick had been left with Lottie for long enough. In any case, there was no rush as far as she was concerned. She knew it would be nearly another week before the ship finally found its way around the Dorset, Hampshire, Sussex and Kent coasts and into its final destination.

9. A stay in London

Both families had received their letters from Charlotte. James and Jane Gosley could scarcely believe what they were reading when the letter, which had been six weeks in delivery, was finally presented to them by the postman. It was Jane who had opened it. Her delight at hearing from her daughter-in-law was first replaced by surprise that her son had not written and then horror. She clutched at her chest and sat down heavily on the nearest chair.

"My God James, Frederick has gone blind also."

"What!!" James stopped in the process of polishing the brass buttons on his coat, his mouth agape.

"It says here James – look!" Jane handed him the letter and then he too had to take a seat.

"And they say lightening never strikes twice!"

"Oh my goodness!" wailed Jane as her tears started, "what are they going to do?"

"Well the first thing I am going to do wife is to find out when the 'British King' is due in port and I'll arrange that the 'Mary Jane' is on hand to pilot her in. "At least I can do that much. It says here that they are to stay with the Adsheads for a while so I daresay they will be all right while he goes and gets checked out at Moorfields. I can't see that taking long – they were not able to do much for Francis," he added pessimistically.

Jane lifted her apron and covered her face with it as she sobbed uncontrollably.

The Tailor's Daughter ~ 111

"What on earth have we done to upset the good Lord?" she cried to nobody in particular.

"Wife!!" exclaimed James, "don't blaspheme." But despite himself he held his head in his hands in despair.

Jane thought it was all too unfair for words. True, she hardly ever saw her boys because they were always away at sea but at least she knew they were happy. However, this was just too much.

All Jane and James could do was continue to worry and fret but it didn't take long for James to find out from the shipping fraternity that the British King was, even now arriving at Plymouth. In a matter of a day she would be arriving in Kent waters and his was the ship that was going to guide her down the Thames to the Albert Docks. At least then he would be able to see his boy if only for a short while, not to mention his daughter-in-law and grandchild.

"I wish I could come too," said Jane wistfully.

"No, you can't come on the pilot ship my dear, but at least this way I know I will see the ship arrive safely into harbour. I'm sure they will be home soon. I can't imagine him wanting to stay in London – he has the salt sea in his veins."

"Not that it will do him much good," retorted Jane as she pummelled the life out of some poor unsuspecting pastry that was destined for a tart, "whoever heard of a blind navigator?"

The conversation ended in a pall of gloom. She couldn't imagine Frederick taking to piano tuning as Francis had done. Not for the first time, she wondered just where she had gone wrong to have two sons struck down with blindness. One thing was sure. James would certainly be helping Frederick with any costs just as he had with Francis.

❖ ❖ ❖

At Chrichton Street, Clapham, the Adshead family were having a similar conversation.

"That nice young man," said Charlotte's mother, "what a shame for this to have happened – poor Charlotte."

She was reading her letter for the umpteenth time but no amount of reading could change her daughter's words.

"We are on our way home mother and father, as poor Frederick is going blind and they can do nothing for him here in New Zealand. It is hoped that they can help him at Moorfields Eye Hospital so I wonder if you would be able to look after us and Lottie for a little while until we sort out what we are going to do.

We miss you and look forward to coming home but wished that it wasn't under these circumstances. We will be arriving on the British King which is the ship I emigrated on four years ago. Give my love to everyone. Love Charlotte and Frederick and baby."

Thomas pushed his glasses up over to the top of his head and went back to the jacket he was tailoring.

"No amount of reading it over and over again is going to make it any different wife." He slung the jacket down again as if he was taking his wrath out on the garment. "We can only look after them as she asks. It is a good thing that most of the older ones have left home or are in service so there will be plenty of room. I'll find out when the British King is due to arrive back home and we shall be there to meet them in a carriage."

"Maybe we should try one of those contraption things", ventured Charlotte Adshead, "Julia's husband has one."

"Oh he would have!" laughed Thomas, momentarily reduced to giggles. "Damn things – horseless carriages they call them. You give me a horse and carriage any day of the week. I want something that is reliable to go and meet them with and not a damned contraption that is no use to anybody and conks out at any given moment."

❖ ❖ ❖

Back on board the British King, most of the passengers had disembarked at Plymouth and now they were slowly making their way through the channel with the Kent coast in the distance. Charlotte dressed Lottie and took her up on deck whilst Frederick made his way to the bridge for, what he knew, would be the last time on any vessel. He could find his way around the ship perfectly well and he didn't need his eyes to tell him where he was and what the different sounds of sirens and horns meant. Moreover, most of the passengers, both second and first class knew him by sight with his white stick and so he was completely comfortable. He knew that from now on there would be so much for Charlotte to see and he needed this time with his old pal Andrew and the other crew members.

"Hello old boy" said Captain Kelly kindly, as he reached the Bridge, "we are just coming along the Kent coast now – I'm expecting the pilot ship to join us any minute."

Frederick could just about make out the shapes of the people around and knew that they would soon be busy making sure that they kept to the right shipping lanes. He knew from his father the importance of piloting these huge vessels in this narrow stretch of water. Suddenly there was a shout from Andrew.

"The pilot ship is just coming alongside Captain."

"Who is it?" said Frederick.

Andrew peered through his binoculars at the little boat that was steaming rapidly towards them.

"It's the 'Mary Jane' old boy, it's the 'Mary Jane'.!"

Andrew and Frederick rushed to the side of the ship and waved frantically.

"The Captain is on deck" said Andrew "big portly chap with a beard like yours."

"That's my father" cried Frederick. He waved as frantically as Andrew but couldn't see what he was waving at.

"He's just gone back into the wheelhouse – let's go and see if he is signalling to the Captain."

They hurried back to the Bridge and sure enough one of the crew was receiving a message in morse code.

"Good sailing my boy, see you in London."

"Signal back" said Frederick, "signal back that we are all fine."

All that remained now was to hurry back to his wife to tell her the news that her father-in-law was even now guiding them safely around the Kent Coast and to the mouth of the Thames and home. She had plenty to think about as she got ready for their arrival home.

She went up on deck and could see the coast, like a long grey line on the horizon. as the huge ship followed the tiny little pilot ship like an enormous elephant following its very tiny master.

Only now was she starting to appreciate the skill and fortitude of these little ships that did such sterling work. A cry from Lottie told her that she needed food. It was time to go below and make sure her baby was looked after. Fresh rations had been put on board both at Tenerife and at Plymouth so nobody starved. There was also a question of sorting out the packing and making sure she looked decent after being away all this time, especially if there was a possibility of seeing her future father-in-law. Meanwhile Frederick paid a visit to the ship's barber to have his hair and whiskers trimmed and she had to go and say farewell to the Cooks she had been helping in the galley. She felt she hadn't been able to do a lot but nevertheless they had appreciated what she did do and there were hugs all round as she bid them farewell.

She went back to the cabin and looked at herself in the mirror. Well, certainly she would not require any rouge – she was as brown as any berry. She looked a little ruefully at her dress. It was hanging on her a little loosely. She had lost some weight – not that she minded that. She could do with losing some but it did make her dress look baggy and she knew that she would be doing some alterations just as soon as she got home. Slowly she got undressed and ready for bed. There would be just a few hours sleep and then they would be in London – her New Zealand adventure over. Maybe, just maybe another adventure would start.

❖ ❖ ❖

It was Lottie that woke Charlotte although it was no surprise given the amount of noise outside the cabin with people running about and doing their last minute preparations.

"Come Charlotte, come and see the ship going down the Thames," cried Frederick, "put the baby in the pram."

She hastily fed her and got her ready and then went up on deck along with crowds of other passengers all anxious to see the sight of the great River Thames, although very little of the water could be seen for the amount of ships coming and going. The little pilot ship was still steadily guiding them along their way amid the sound of horns and hooters and sirens. She gave thanks that it was a lovely sunny day but felt so sorry for Frederick as he tried to peer into the void that was his failing eyesight. However, already he was learning to live with it despite the bitter blow, although she knew that much of the time he was putting on a brave face for her.

"I wonder if your parents will be there to meet us?" he queried.

"Of course they bloomin' well will" said Charlotte in her best cockney accent. He never failed to be charmed by it.

Many of the passengers had found seats on deck. It would be quite a while before the ship got to the Albert Docks but all Charlotte and Frederick wanted to do was to just stand their and hold on to the rail whilst little Lottie was the centre of attention for anyone who passed by.

"Oh what a lovely child" cooed one elderly lady, "such a long journey for so young."

She was just grateful that she had been able to keep her clean and she had no real illnesses on board and sent up a silent prayer of thanks.

Now she was starting to recognise the familiar skyline of London with the wharfs and the cranes. People were starting to gather on deck with their luggage and all along the vast ship there were ripples of laughter and cheering and people exchanging addresses as they prepared to part company.

❖ ❖ ❖

In the much smaller 'Mary Jane' James Gosley was also taking in the sights and sounds. He had slept for a short while during which time his First Mate had taken over. Now with a bowl of porridge inside him he was ready to take the helm. The 'Mary Jane' under his stewardship guided the enormous 'British King' into the Albert Docks past other equally enormous ships which were already in their berths and then, with a final signal to

Captain Kelly he gave instructions to his engine room to increase speed.

"Now they are on their own" he said "that's our job done boys. All I want to do now is moor up and get on board that thing behind us."

The little ship sped away with its crew of twelve men and in no time at all they had moored up in a small tributary off the main dock. James put on his peaked hat and smoothed his uniform down.

"You get off and have a well earned beer at the 'King's Head'" he shouted to his crew. "I'll join you when I have seen my son."

With that he was off towards the main dockside just in time to see the 'British King' come alongside. It would take some time to drop the anchor and get the ship properly moored before passengers could safely disembark but there were crowds of people there and a band playing lustily. It would have been a momentous occasion had not the reason for the homecoming been so sad.

James Morehouse Gosley was a familiar face among the officials at the dockside and so was able to get on board via the crew gangplank long before the main gangplanks were lowered in three separate places along the ship. Andrew was waiting for him at the top and put out a helpful arm to assist him aboard.

"Welcome Captain Gosley," He smiled and put his arm out in a flamboyant gesture. "Welcome to our little ship."

James laughed. "Little! I'll stick to the 'Mary Jane' if you don't mind my boy. What a thunderous great thing this is."

"Come quickly" said Andrew, "I'll show you where your boy is. It's quicker to go down a deck and go along the second class deck – that way we will miss the crowds."

118 ~ *The Tailor's Daughter*

The pair ran down the steps and quickly rushed along almost the full length of the vessel to the stern – a distance of over one hundred feet. They went past the cabins and then up the steps to where the second class and steerage passengers were crowding to catch their first sight of loved ones. Andrew and James spotted Frederick at the same time, standing out in the crowd with his white stick over his arm. Then a second later they saw Charlotte with the baby and Rose standing together.

"Frederick, Frederick my boy" shouted James. Frederick knew that voice anywhere.

"Father!" They fell into each others arms while Charlotte and Andrew looked on. Very few of the assembled company had a dry eye.

"My boy, my boy!" James tried to keep a stiff upper lip but found it exceedingly difficult. Then he turned to Charlotte.... "and this is the lovely lady – and, my lovely grandchild" He was caught between happiness and despair, and also annoyance because he knew this was but a fleeting visit. He had to get back to his crew and take the ship back to Deal.

The band struck up a rousing tune again and everybody began to leave the ship. There were hugs for people they had met on board and then Andrew had to leave.

"Jobs to do Freddy old boy, jobs to do." He grinned. "I'll see you again – I can't see you staying away from the sea air for long."

It was the first hint that Charlotte got that, no – she could not imagine Frederick being content to stay in London. Andrew was right – the sea air was in his blood. One only had to look at his old salt of a father who was just an older version of him though a lot portlier. There were more hugs all round and then Andrew went on his way leaving the little group to disembark.

The Tailor's Daughter ~ 119

Gradually the crowds on the quayside were disappearing which made it easier for Charlotte to suddenly catch sight of her parents. Thomas and Charlotte were patiently waiting at the entrance to the disembarkation hall.

James and a member of the crew helped them ashore and for the first time in nearly two months Charlotte felt her feet hit terra firma.

"Mother, Father!" she cried as she ran towards them, Lottie bouncing in the pram. Once again there were more hugs and James Gosley met his son's mother and father-in-law for the first time. That was all he was able to do though – just meet them. No sooner had he said hello than he had to take his leave. He couldn't expect his crew to wait for him for ever and he knew Frederick would come home just as soon as he could. He already knew from Charlotte's letter that the plan was for the little family to stay at Clapham until he had been to Moorfields.

"You just come home as soon as you can my boy," he said "you can't impose on these good people for ever – we have plenty of room at Deal"

"Nah, don't you worry my old china!" said Thomas, "we'll look after them." He put his arm around his daughter while his wife cooed away at the baby. "Cor blimey Charlotte, you look as though you could do with some meat on you."

"We didn't eat much on board," she laughed, "anyway, it will do me good."

James turned to his son.

"Frederick my boy, I am sure things will be all right."

"They weren't with Francis," he replied.

"This might be different. They can do such wondrous things these days."

Even as he said it James knew that he sounded unconvincing but he vowed that he would look after his son and do whatever he could for the family. At the same time Thomas Adshead was thinking the same.

"I'm glad I've seen you Frederick," said James "and your mother will be pleased to know that you are in high spirits. Now I have to take my leave and get back to the Mary Jane. We have to leave on the afternoon tide," He put some sovereigns in Frederick's hand and thumped him on the back. "You let me know if you need any more my boy – whatever it takes."

Charlotte gulped. He seemed such a lovely old man. She somehow knew she was doing the right thing in not telling him about the death of little James. How could she make him sad?

There were more tearful farewells and the family were then left in the care of the Adsheads. Thomas took control.

"Come on, there are plenty of cabs about with good horses that have not yet been frightened off the road by blinkin' contraptions. We will be home in no time."

❖ ❖ ❖

10. New Horizons

Charlotte sat in the waiting room of the Moorfields Eye Hospital which was a short cab ride from her parent's house in Clapham. This was their third visit over the past few weeks and she felt as though she knew every facet of the room. Even now Frederick was visiting yet another eye specialist but all seemed to come out with the same answer. That there was not a lot they could do. She thanked God for the fact that they had her parents and she was also very grateful for the fact that most of her sisters were now either married or in service. At least there was plenty of room and with her mother occupied, and enjoying, looking after Lottie, she was able to make herself useful by helping her father in the tailoring shop. It was a business that was doing very well and Charlotte herself was no mean seamstress. Moreover Thomas had invested in a modern treadle sewing machine which enabled him to achieve many more stitches and designs. There was a constant stream of toffs coming and going to the front room of the large house and he was never short of work.

   It was homely and comfortable but she knew they couldn't impose on her family for ever. Also she had a shrewd suspicion that she was pregnant again. Much as she loved children this could not have come at a worse time.

   She sat patiently and browsed through a copy of the Times that had been left on the side table of the waiting room. There was a large article about the New Zealand earthquake and drawings of the aftermath and the devastation. She recognised

122 ~ *The Tailor's Daughter*

some of the area and again wondered about Jenny and James Braithwaite. There was a lot to read in the Times, stories about Prince Edward and his antics and even photographs. There was a real photograph of Queen Victoria that had been taken for her Jubilee a few years earlier. Charlotte still found it difficult to comprehend that you could have an actual image of a person and not a drawing. There was also a large photograph of Lord Salisbury, the Prime Minister though she could not agree with the idea that only men could elect him. It annoyed her immensely that she was not allowed to vote but, like many things, she had to live with it. She found herself wondering what life would be like in a few years time. Already so many things were changing. There were more contraptions on the road, as her father called them, and the invention of the telephone.

She was disturbed from her train of thought by the emergence of Frederick once again accompanied by an earnest looking doctor. Her husband looked grim and was clearly not very happy with what he had been told.

"There's nothing they can do Charlotte." He sat down on the chair at the side of her and waved a bottle in the air. "They have given me these drops to put in my eyes, but they don't have much hope. The Wellington doctor was right, it is glaucoma and the most I can hope is that it won't get any worse."

Her heart sank but she put on a brave face.

"Well we shall just have to adapt" she replied. "We have done it before and look how good you were at finding your way around the ship. If you can do it with that you can do it again with other things. We *will* get that guesthouse one day and we will start making plans just as soon as we get home.

"Damn it Charlotte" he cried, "what was the point in coming all this way home? We might just as well have stopped in New Zealand."

The doctor looked on sympathetically as she put her arm around him.

"Now husband, think what you are saying" she said kindly, "if we had not come home we would have been forced to wonder for the rest of our lives if anything could have been done. At least we made the effort and now we know for sure."

"In any case Mr. Gosley" interjected the doctor, "as I said to you, it may not get any worse than it is now."

"Drat it, it can't get much worse!"

"Come on Frederick" said Charlotte, "we have to plan our future."

For the millionth time Frederick wondered just what he would have done without his wife and already felt comforted as they made their way down the endless corridors and out to the outside world. Charlotte thanked the doctor and hailed a cab.

"One thing is certain my dear" said Frederick, "we have imposed on your parents for long enough. We must get to Deal and let my mother see her grandchild."

Charlotte resisted the temptation to tell him that she might have a grandchild that she did not bargain for. She would have to wait until she was sure, but, perhaps if it were a boy she would feel less guilty about not telling them about baby James.

Their dilemma was resolved by the very unlikely source of Charlotte's sister Julia. Julia and her husband Wilfred were paying a visit and there was much to talk about. There were plenty of adults to keep the children out of mischief and so the two girls caught up on four years of gossip. Julia was anxious to know all about New Zealand and Charlotte wanted to hear about her sister's life as a married lady living by the seaside at Eastbourne in Sussex. Wilfred worked in offices there as a Tea Agent and they had settled in a large house near the sea front.

"It's the place to be for people to take the air" said Julia, "I love London but it has become so congested with horses and, now, this new fangled motor car thing."

"I would like to run a Lodging House" said Charlotte but it will be a long time before we have the money; besides".... she lent towards Julia and whispered, "I think I have another baby on the way."

The two girls giggled and the conversation moved on to other things like the latest fashions and hair styles while Wilfred buried his head in the newspaper of the day.

Charlotte still wore her hair rolled up and pinned all around her head. Normally her hair fell all the way down to her waist and it was becoming increasingly difficult to keep in enough pins to avoid it falling everywhere. Julia, on the other hand, wore her hair much shorter and it was far less trouble.

"Oh I can't spend time in front of the mirror any more" she said, "and it is really not the thing to have it loose like some young girl, so I had it chopped off. It is so much easier."

If Charlotte did have another child on the way she too could do with a simpler style and decided, like Julia, that drastic action needed to be taken.

It was their mother who first came into the room in time to see her daughter's hair all over the floor and Julia wielding the scissors.

"Oh daughters!" cried the older lady "what are you doing? Charlotte, all that lovely hair my child."

"Mother, from now on I am going to be even busier than I have been in the past – I won't have the time to stand for ever putting pins in. You know how easily they fall out."

Her dark hair was now just to shoulder length, just long enough to curl it up in a small bun at the back of her head. She looked ruefully at her hair all over the floor.

"Maybe we could stuff a cushion with it mother?"

"I think you will need a bit more than even yours to stuff a cushion my dear," she replied. She gave Charlotte a hug and brushed up the offending hair and the conversation returned to the dilemma of her daughter and son-in-law's future. Suddenly there was a rustle of the newspaper and Wilfred's head appeared over the top.

"They could always go to an Agency and get a tenancy" he ventured. "Eastbourne is becoming very popular with the gentry now and I am sure that they could get an establishment with the sort of references that they must have."

Julia could always rely on Wilfred to say something sensible.

"You could come and stay with us" said Julia "and visit the Agency in the town."

"I must admit I do miss the sea already" said Frederick, "but what on earth could I do – I can't even pilot a ship like my father." He thumped his fist down on the table which made the cups rattle.

"In fact I am no use to man nor beast!" he cried, "no use to man nor beast."

Thomas came into the room with a tape measure around his neck and his spectacles on the end of his nose. He reacted angrily.

"I don't want to hear you say such a thing again son-in-law, do you hear me? You are every use and I think it's an excellent idea."

"If all else fails husband, you can look after the children while I go out to work" said Charlotte.

Frederick immediately felt sorry but he could certainly see where his wife got her spirit from!

The following day they waved a fond farewell to Julia and Wilfred and promised them that they would look into the possibility of moving to Eastbourne.

"That is, after we have been to Deal" said Frederick. "I think my parents have been patient for long enough."

Charlotte could not help feeling that she was about to embark on yet another adventure.

❖ ❖ ❖

Frederick, Charlotte and Lottie travelled down to Deal by train and were enthusiastically welcomed by Jane and James to their house. It was a new lease of life for Frederick to get the smell of the sea in his nostrils again and he tried to be as much help to his father as somebody who was almost blind could be. The drops had worked inasmuch as things did not get any worse, but then as Frederick said whilst in the eye hospital – "there wasn't much room for getting any worse!"

It was also nice to receive letters from Francis who was up in Scotland. They were of course written by his wife Andria, and Charlotte replied on behalf of Frederick.

Soon it was apparent that she was indeed pregnant again and for a while they all remained comfortable in James's four bedroom house. There was plenty of room now that all the children had fled the nest and James did not mind having more mouths to feed. He was just delighted to have his son home.

However, Frederick began to get restless. They had a visit to Eastbourne on the train to see Julia and Wilfred leaving Lottie with Jane. They could see that Julia had been right. This seaside resort was the place to be, with its tall clean Georgian buildings and the fresh sea air that did not smell of fish as it tended to do in Deal. The idea of moving there was very tempting.,

"I can't be idle for the rest of my life Father," said Frederick when they were together on their own. "I have to do something and if Wilfred can give me a job perhaps we could rent a place and take in lodgers. It has to be the answer, and now that Charlotte is pregnant again I need to earn a living."

James felt that his son was right, although he failed to understand how he could be a Tea Agent or even help Wilfred in that capacity. He did know though that he had never brought any of his children up to be idle and therefore he would not stand in his son's way.

"You do what you have to do my boy," he patted him on the shoulder, "you do what you have to do and with my blessing."

Charlotte was happy to go to Eastbourne. She got on exceedingly well with Jane but she needed her own space to bring up her own children and if they went to live with Julia and Wilfred for a short while then that would be one step in the right direction.

It was decided that they would take as little luggage as possible and send for it once they were settled, which clearly would not be until after the baby was born. She looked in the mirror at her ever expanding waist – she would be glad when it was all over, though it was a bit daunting to have two small children *and* a blind husband *and* run a lodging house.

Baby Mary was born in Julia's house at Eastbourne. Fortunately Wilfred was quite well placed and it was a large rambling mansion in the centre of town with plenty of room both for his own family and his sister-in-law's rapidly growing brood.

Charlotte couldn't help but feel a little pang of disappointment that the baby had turned out to be a girl. She knew how much Frederick's father would have liked a grandson to carry on the family name. How could she tell him that there had been one but that he had barely lasted a couple of days? Despite the fact that she knew that it was all to common she still felt mildly guilty at the way things had worked out, but they were all getting old and there was no need to upset them after all this time.

Once Charlotte was on her feet again she put on her best dress and hat and made sure that Frederick visited the barbers before calling at the Agency to see what properties there were available. She had references from Lord Brownlow and from Mr and Mrs Braithwaite as well as Frederick's certificate as First Mate on the British Empire. She just hoped that it was impressive enough. She was ready for the first question which she knew would come.

"How can you run a lodging house with a blind husband?" said the elderly looking man behind the desk.

"All we want for the time being is somewhere to rent" said Charlotte patiently. "With my husband's pension and his work for my brother-in-law we will manage until we obtain lodgers."

"Well we do have a place in Marine Road near the sea front. I can get my boy to show you it if you wish." He rang a bell on his desk and a young lad came in looking very smart in a frock coat and knee breeches.

"Show this lady and gentleman to that establishment in Marine Road." He gave the lad the keys and the threesome made their way the short distance to the house.

What confronted them was a three story edifice larger than they had envisaged.

"It's huge," said Charlotte as they looked around. "I just hope we can get enough lodgers to make it pay."

Frederick tried with what minute amount of eyesight he had left to see around the place and feel his way but if Charlotte liked it then that was good enough for him.

"We'll shake on it my man" he said "and we will be in to the office immediately to pay the first months rent."

The Gosley family moved into 3 Marine Road, Eastbourne as the last rays of an Indian summer shimmered across the sea and Frederick started his work as a Tea Agent with Wilfred.

It was all a bit daunting at first but everyone tried to make things easy for him and with the use of an abacus he was able to work out the tariffs on the supplies of tea coming in from abroad and being shipped onward to London and all points around the British Isles.

He was under no illusions though, no one else would have employed him and Wilfred had the patience of a Saint. In truth it was quite a depressing and uninspiring job and a far cry from his life at sea but it would have been churlish to be too miserable and show any lack of appreciation. After all it paid the rent.

The hope was though that with paying lodgers he would be able to cut down on his hours working with Wilfred and spend more time at home helping Charlotte. The little ones were growing fast and becoming a real handful and with the extra work that would be involved with the guests another pair of hands would be needed even though the eyes failed.

At last, though, they did seem to be settled. The New Zealand adventure was well and truly over. Now followed another adventure – that of bringing up their children and making a go of the Lodging House!

House in Marine Road

❖ ❖ ❖

It wasn't long before they had their first lodger but it was one that was totally unexpected. Charlotte had just tucked Lottie and Mary into bed and it was she who first heard the knock on the door and a very familiar voice.

"Oi, come on you two, let the dog see the rabbit!"

They both looked at each other at the same time and Mary was unceremoniously dumped in her crib.

"Andrew!" they both exclaimed with one voice.

"What the devil....!" cried Frederick and a smile came across his face that Charlotte had not seen in a very long while. Despite his lack of sight he was at the door before his wife and there was their friend, looking brown and weather beaten and very pleased with himself for surprising them.

"How did you know we were here?" laughed Charlotte as she hugged him and gave him a kiss.

"Your parents my dear – I came in on the 'British King' two weeks ago and called on them in Clapham."

He was still standing on the doorstep as nobody had moved to one side. The couple were rooted to the spot. It was Mary's cries that brought them back down to earth.

"Come in, come in my man!" said Frederick "put the kettle on woman!"

Andrew followed them into the house and watched as Charlotte put the kettle on the big kitchen range. Frederick deftly picked the crying Mary up and soothed her.

"Well I can see you have been getting on with it," laughed Andrew and nodded in the direction of Mary. Even as he spoke Lottie appeared at the door – a little sleepy eyed toddler in her white night clothes and very puzzled as to what all the noise and chaos was about. It took a cup of hot chocolate to persuade her to go back to bed.

"Off you go now young lady," laughed Andrew, "I'll play with you tomorrow because I hope..." he looked at Charlotte, "I hope I shall be able to impose on you and stay the night."

"You can stay as long as you like old boy," interjected Frederick, Charlotte took the children and settled them into bed again while her husband pressed Andrew further.

"Come on, tell all, what are you doing here, how is everyone on the British King, how is the Captain..."

"Oi, first things first" smiled Andrew, "I am here because, like you, I have found a good woman."

"Well done old boy," Frederick stood up again and slapped him on the back.

"Yes, I married her on my last trip down to the Antipodes." He turned to Charlotte who had just come downstairs after pacifying Mary. "I think you know her?" He grinned wickedly. "Your friend Harriet."

"Harriet?" my Harriet?"

"The very same the beauty with the flaming red hair that came with you back in '84'"

"Oh Andrew, how very lovely, how did that happen?"

Frederick speedily took his tea away as efficiently as a man with sight.

"We can do better than that old boy – lets open up something stronger Charlotte dear!

"It was a hasty affair," Andrew explained as Charlotte poured out some rum. "I always liked her but met her again when I went back – fell like a fish on a line and we married on the last trip."

"But where is she?" cried Charlotte, "why isn't she here with us?"

"I only came back to England to tie up a few loose ends and visit the shipping company because..... " he paused for effect. "I am going back as an immigrant and I am going to take up sheep farming."

"Sheep farming?" Charlotte and Frederick said it in unison.

"Yes, like you Freddy old chap, I have done my share on the oceans of the world. It's time to settle down now and raise a

The Tailor's Daughter ~ 133

family. Harriet's employer runs a sheep farm and has offered to take me on."

Charlotte felt sad at the idea that Andrew would not be coming back but she kept it to herself. It was wonderful news and Harriet was a nice girl.

Andrew started to rummage around in his pocket and pulled out a crumpled looking letter.

"Almost forgot in all the excitement," he said "got a letter for you from Jenny Braithwaite."

"Oh my goodness" cried Charlotte and clutched at the letter. She had so wanted to know how they had got on in the dreadful 1988 earthquake.

"I'm afraid it has taken a long time to get to you. She gave it to me in Lyttleton just before I left." He paused and looked serious for a minute. "Terrible damage there don't you know – must have frightened everyone to death. Lots of repairs needed to the 'Sailor's Return.'"

"Did she get my letter?" asked Charlotte cutting him short.

"Yes, she gave the reply to me as she did not know where you would be. I promised I would call on your parents."

Charlotte opened the letter and read it out loud so that Frederick could hear it:

> *"My dear Charlotte and Frederick, I hope you are both well and that little Lottie is keeping well too. We also hope that Frederick was able to get some comfort at the Eye hospital. I expect you heard all about our earthquake soon after you left. It was dreadful. It felt as though the whole world was shaking and the ground opened up in many places. The ships were tossed around the harbour like corks. Many of the wooden buildings were raised to the ground and the tremors were heard as far away as Wellington. The 'Sailor's Return' had all its windows shattered and some*

structural damage but nothing that can not be repaired. Thank the lord that there were no deaths although plenty of injuries due to flying glass and wood. I still love the country though and the scenery, as you know, is always breathtaking. I'm still able to sit at the front door and watch all the ships down in the harbour and as long as I can do that I am happy.

James is keeping well although he is always moaning about something, but you know James. He has always got to have something to moan about. The British King is in port now and so I daresay Andrew will be here before long. It's such wonderful news that he has found a nice young lady in Harriet.. I shall give this letter to him and wish them both joy and peace. Take good care of yourselves and love to your family. Your loving friends, Jenny and James xx

Charlotte brushed a tear from her eye. She missed Jenny but it was with a considerable amount of relief that she read that they had got through the earthquake almost unscathed. She could hear Lottie chattering away to herself upstairs and gave thanks to God.

"Dang me though Andrew," exclaimed Frederick when she had finished reading. "Don't these freaks of nature put the wind up you? I don't think I fancy the ground opening up under my feet."

"It's a chance we are prepared to take old boy," replied Andrew, "New Zealand is such a lovely country and there are such opportunities there we want to give it a go." He laughed at the look on Charlotte's face. "It's not like earthquakes are happening every day of the week."

The three talked until late and it was Charlotte who finally looked at the clock. She had the little girls to get up for in the morning. She bid her goodnights and left the two old pals enjoying their gossip. It had been a very long time indeed since she had seen Frederick so animated. She wondered how he would cope with being cooped up in an office all day.

The following day Andrew had to move on and go about his business. He had much to do before taking his last trip on the British King. Charlotte cooked him a hearty breakfast and watched as he laughed and joked with the children. Two year old Lottie giggled and rewarded him with beaming smiles, while one year old Mary was more concerned about sucking her thumb.

"Lovely kids Charlotte" he smiled, "wait until you have got a few more eh!" He winked in the direction of Frederick.

Charlotte blushed but she was used to Andrew and his quips.

The discussion ended in laughter and hugs and kisses as Andrew put his knapsack on his back. He looked down ruefully at his seaman's jacket which was festooned in brass buttons.

"Guess I shall be trading this in for a sheep shearer's apron." He grinned. Then he cocked his peaked cap on his head and they watched him walk down the road and out of their lives. They would be unlikely to see him again.

Now it was time to get on with their own lives and try and make the lodging house pay its way.

❖ ❖ ❖

11. The Lodging House

In fact it wasn't long before the Agency started to recommend lodgers and Charlotte was able to let out the upstairs rooms. Each lodger brought in as much as three shillings per day and greatly supplemented the household budget. It enabled Frederick to just work for Wilfred for three mornings a week and the rest of the time he assisted in the organisation of the business and working out the tax returns. It even left a little time to enjoy the fresh sea air of Eastbourne and the delights of the comparatively new Pier and Pavilion.

With what little time Charlotte had spare she made clothes with her trusty sewing machine. She often mused that it would be the first thing she would grab if ever there were a fire! Lottie and Mary seemed to grow an inch a day but it was a treat to have both of them out of napkins and using the privy in a proper manner. Of course she had to help but, all in all, things seemed to be working out well with occasional visits from her parents. With two daughters living in Eastbourne and their ever growing collection of grandchildren it didn't take much persuading for Thomas and Charlotte Adshead to come down on the train, although Thomas could never bring himself to travel from the station in 'one of those contraptions' as he still insisted on calling the ever popular motor car.

And so as a new decade began, and the 1890s became a reality, all was well in the Gosley household. Charlotte was actually able to count her blessings. The lodgers, usually young men, kept themselves to themselves and as soon as one moved on to pastures new the Agency found another to take their place.

Most of the young men were having a last minute break at an English seaside before going off to the Boer War. There seemed to be so many losing their lives and it was possible to read all about it in The Times. Charlotte didn't really understand what it was all about – all this talk about the Orange Free State and the Transvaal. She seemed to remember that there had been a similar confrontation with the Boers ten years previously when she had been working in Cambridge for Lord Brownlow. History seemed to be repeating itself. All she could do was pray that these young men would return safely. Of course she had no idea that in less than fourteen years time there would be a war to end all wars and in which millions would die.

❖ ❖ ❖

Much as she missed the streets of London Charlotte enjoyed the sea air and had no regrets about moving to Eastbourne. The freshness and the sea smells reminded her of Lyttleton Harbour but there any similarity ended. The scenery had been breathtaking and the mostly wooden dwellings seemed to fit in with the background as if they had been there for centuries. Also, of course, the harbour had been seething with ships of all shapes and sizes. Here, at Eastbourne, it was more a holiday resort and the houses lining the esplanade were of stone. There was very little time to go down to the beach, but if ever Frederick 'went missing' that is where he would always be found.

It was difficult for him. She was convinced that Wilfred had manufactured the job as a Tea Agent for him and Frederick only worked there a few hours a week. The rest of the time he spent in helping her with all the work needed to run a guest house. There were times though when he got so frustrated with himself that he would lose his temper and then feel very sorry afterwards. After all it wasn't Charlotte's or the children's fault that he had lost his eyesight and had to cut short his New Zealand plans.

The one thing he was good at though was sums. Despite his disability he could add and subtract numbers in his head and, with the help of an abacus, he could do the accounts for the family as well as working out the figures for the tariffs on the tea for Wilfred and his employers. He had proved, as long as you could add up you would never be out of work. It was a different philosophy to Charlotte's father who believed that you needed to sew or cook to always be employed.

❖ ❖ ❖

Having given birth to three children in the space of three years Charlotte was quite grateful that for the next three years there was no sign of any pregnancy. The more the toddlers ran her ragged then the more she wondered how her mother managed with nine of them. Mind you, as with most families at the time, by the time the youngest were born the oldest were out at work. Also, her mother did not have a blind husband and therefore did not have to worry about keeping everything in its place.

"As long as nothing is moved" she told the little girls "then your father will find his way around."

It was difficult for toddlers to understand though and there were many times when Frederick would trip over something and curse.

"Frederick!" Charlotte would exclaim, "there is a child in the room."

It came as a relief when Lottie was old enough to start school. For a while there was a brief respite. The lodgers were no trouble at all. She made them breakfast in the morning and they were gone for the day. Then, no sooner had one set of lodgers paid their bills and gone then it was a case of everybody giving a hand to change the bedding and clean the rooms ready for the next lot of guests and the sheets went off to the laundry.

It was a shame that they had to come back from New Zealand but there was no good 'crying over spilt milk'. It was done and they had some lovely memories to look back on. It was a regret that she would never get to see again some of the people she had met there though. They had all emigrated for a reason – to make a new life. But it was funny how things worked out. Who knows, if she had not gone in the first place she might still be at the Brownlow's in Cambridge and she never would have met Frederick. In fact, she might never have got married and her children would never have existed which would have affected every generation to come! It was quite a thought!

The main thing for Frederick was the sea. He had worked hard to become a First Mate and it was wicked that he could no longer continue in a job that he loved, but at least Charlotte had been happy to come to the seaside. He just loved to sit on the sea wall and listen to the waves on the shingle and the cries of the seagulls as they fought over a piece of bread. He had precious little sight left at all now. He had religiously used the drops given to him by the hospital but they had only put off the inevitable. He could see a shape if somebody came up close to him but that was all and even that was slowly diminishing. It had been five years now though and he had to get used to it. Being a ship's navigator had to be confined to his memories.

❖ ❖ ❖

Henry Francis Gosley was born in the spring of 1893. Charlotte had enjoyed a three year rest from breast feeding and napkins but all that had come to an end with the arrival of their little boy. Everyone was absolutely thrilled that at last there was a boy to carry on the family name. Thankfully the other children could use the privy properly and so the washing was not as irksome as it might have been and she even managed to find time to do some tailoring with the sewing machine given to her by her father. This brought in a little more money for the growing family.

A wonderful new gadget where babies were concerned, was the invention of the safety pin! Some genius had developed a pin that could be used to fasten a napkin securely instead of bothering with tie ups. It was safe to use as it had a special function that closed down on the point once closed. Charlotte thought this was a marvellous thing and decided that there were some things about the 1890s that she really did approve of! When she was able to buy her first safety pins from the Drapers in town she guarded them as if they had been made of silver.

There had also been the invention of towelling which made napkins far more absorbent and so things were improving all the time. For all that, Charlotte rarely had a quiet moment to herself and she often wondered how on earth previous generations coped.

She was also exceedingly relieved to have a boy. He would never replace little James in her heart but he would be loved just the same and finally, James Morehouse Gosley Senior would have his long awaited grandson.

❖ ❖ ❖

The Tailor's Daughter ~ 141

In London Thomas Adshead was becoming increasingly annoyed with the contraptions that seemed to be taking over the streets.

"Dang it Charlotte" he said to his wife one day, "I have had enough of this – I'm too old to cope with all this modern stuff replacing the horses. Why I just escaped with my life crossing the road."

He was pushing sixty five now. Not old by most people's standards, but a lifetime of cigars and whiskey was beginning to take its toll. Besides, London was becoming increasingly polluted. It was bad enough with tons of horse dung but now the smells from these dratted engines were very testing. The couple had already talked at length about moving to live near the seaside and now, with the arrival of yet another grandchild and two daughters living at Eastbourne Thomas felt he would like to end his days breathing in the sea air.

His wife was of two minds. She had been born in the countryside of Wiltshire but had spent all her married life in London. She had grown used to it, but the children had gone now with only young Annie left. It had been a great disruption when her daughter had gone off to New Zealand and an even greater one when she had come back with a child and a blind husband. Now Charlotte had three children and the older lady wanted to see more of them.

It had been exciting living in London though and she too was sorry to see the demise of the horse drawn carriage in favour of these spluttering contraptions.

Only a month ago there had been huge activity in London when Prince George married Mary of Teck at St. James's Palace. They had travelled over to the area of Buckingham Palace and had stood in the crowd to see the procession of landaus as they brought the couple and their entourage from the Church to the reception. They even got a glimpse of the old Queen Victoria. It was a grand occasion indeed and Charlotte did wonder if the same grandness could ever be achieved with a 'contraption' instead of a landau pulled along by beautiful horses.

Thomas had done well with his tailoring business but larger companies were taking over and making clothes in bulk and less people required a personal tailor. The huge cotton mills in the North were supplying stores such as the comparatively newly established Harrods. He realised that he would need to make a quick sale whilst the business was still a successful concern. He was, therefore, able to sell the lot along with the house for a tidy sum.

He did keep his precious sewing machines but, other than that, he figured that he would have enough money in the Bank to be able to retire, provide for his wife and live comfortably until the 'great tailor in the skies' came and called for him.

Therefore, to the great pride and joy of their daughters the couple moved 'lock stock and barrel to Eastbourne where they secured a comfortable three bedroom semi detached house not far from the sea front in Compton Terrace.

The younger Charlotte was delighted and so, on the face of it anyway, things were ticking along very well indeed, with only the occasional regret that she was not able to continue her adventure in New Zealand. Salt was rubbed into the wound by a letter from Andrew.

It was still two months to get a letter from that part of the world and so most of the news was out of date but she was always thrilled to hear from him and Harriet. She read it out to Frederick.

> *Dear Charlotte and Frederick,*
>
> *I hope this finds you keeping well and that those delightful children are growing big and strong. The weather here is brilliant sunshine and everywhere looks beautiful. I finally got my little smallholding and we have twenty sheep. Not many I know, but if nature does its job then this will increase. I have already had a go at shearing although Harriet's old boss had to help me. It was as if the sheep had a dozen legs and all kicking at me. I expect I shall get the hang of it all one day.*
>
> *By the time you receive this we will have had our first child. Harriet is getting bigger by the minute but is keeping well and has me waiting on her of course!*

"Wait until he has got a couple more!" laughed Frederick. Charlotte ignored him and carried on reading.

> *Jenny and James send their love. The Sailor's Return is as busy as ever and still the immigrants keep coming. The Harbour is always full of boats and they are a grand sight. Nevertheless, we do miss our old homeland but I am enjoying learning new skills. I don't miss the sailing days too much. At least the ground stays firm most of the time and one thing is for sure, we are never short of mutton or wool. Look after yourselves and God bless.*
>
> *Andrew and Harriet.*

She wiped a tear from her eye. Frederick didn't see it. Life had to go on and she had a stew to prepare.

❖ ❖ ❖

12. (1899) Big Changes

Charlotte held on to Frederick's arm and placed her other arm around the shoulders of Lottie as, together with the rest of the family, they watched the coffin containing the remains of Jane Gosley being lowered into the grave in St. Georges Cemetery, Deal. The sunny autumn day belied the miserable feelings of everyone there. It had only been a few months ago back in the Spring that they had gone through the same procedure with her husband, James Morehouse Gosley and stood in exactly the same place. On that occasion half of Deal had been there, together with scores of sailors from the Cinque Port little ships. They had all come to pay their respects to the old man who had followed generations before him in guiding, firstly the great sailing vessels and latterly the modern steel hulled great monsters that were driven by engines as well as sail.

"They had a good life" Frederick whispered.

"I think your mother died of a broken heart," whispered Charlotte.

Most people at James's funeral did not expect Jane to survive him for long. She was frail and beside herself with grief. However, nobody had expected her demise to be quite so soon and that they would be back here again. There were fewer people in numbers for this second funeral but it was none the less dignified and none the less sad.

Lottie and Mary stood side by side both consumed by sadness. They had visited their grandparents on numerous occasions and had grown very attached to them. Young Henry, who was still only six, barely understood what was going on but he stood like a man and held the hand of the latest addition to the family, young Frederick who was just three and wondered what all the fuss was about. Frederick was a dear little chap but a bit of a handful especially as Charlotte was hoping that, once and for all, she would have no more nappies, or breast feeding after Henry. She had made up her mind that Henry Francis would be her last. But there was no accounting for nature! In fact, he was a welcome edition and the girls made a fuss of him but he was an added burden which, in some ways, they could well do without. The house was crowded enough with the lodgers which they needed to make the place pay it's way. True, Lottie would be 'put out to service' soon, but it would be some while before Mary was old enough.

Both Charlotte and Frederick thought that there might be some inheritance to come their way once Jane died, but they would rather have been poor and have her alive, and just now, finances could not have been further from Frederick's thoughts. This part of the funeral procedure seemed so final.

Charlotte, on the other hand, was barely aware of the Vicar saying the words of committal as the coffin was lowered into the ground but she knew that things would never be the same again, especially if any inheritance should come their way. She also had certain misgivings which invaded her thoughts as she tried to concentrate on the solemn occasion. For ages Frederick had persisted in the notion that they needed to expand the business and have even more paying guests and frankly, Charlotte did not think they could cope. But still, she would cross that bridge when she came to it. Just at the moment there was a funeral to concentrate on and she channelled her thoughts in that direction as the final handful of soil was thrown on the coffin lid and the assembled company turned and walked away. It was so final, so sad, and the end of an era.

Amid a sea of grief there was one bonus. The death of both their mother and father in such a short space of time had brought Francis and Andria back from Scotland for a while.

They would be staying with Frederick's sister Jane Whaley until all the necessary procedures had been dealt with and it gave them the opportunity to get together with the rest of the family. Jane was their older sister by a couple of years and she was there with her husband Henry. Henry travelled around quite a lot as he was employed as a stationery salesman.

It was very poignant and emotional to see both brothers together and talking to each other with unseeing eyes as they made their way back to the house in Victoria Road where James and Jane had spent their final years.

"Well, its the end of an era old boy!" said Francis as his sister, 'young' Jane poured both himself and Frederick a sherry. "It's the end of an era."

"I wonder what will happen to the 'Mary Jane'?" said Charlotte.

"Oh the solicitors will see to that," said Frederick, "I expect there will be somebody from the crew who will want to buy it."

"Oh it's the end of an era!" said Francis again, unconsciously repeating himself for a third time.

"Father had seen so many changes." Frederick's older brother James joined in the conversation. "Just think that he started when it was all sail and now we have engines."

"I remember when it was all sail," Frederick reminded him. "How I miss those days."

"Never mind, Queen Victoria goes on and on doesn't she!" Francis felt for his glass and picked it up. "Come on, let's have

The Tailor's Daughter ~ 147

one for the Queen." He raised his glass in the air not realising that he had already drunk most of it.

"The Queen, God bless her," they all chanted in unison. It was unusual for all three brothers to be together. Francis was usually, of course, up in Scotland and the older man, James, spent most of his time at sea going backwards and forwards to America and the colonies. Frederick couldn't help but think that if his little James had lived then history would be truly repeating itself with his three little boys. As it was he could hear Henry and Frederick Jnr arguing the toss over something. It reminded him so much of the old days when the three brothers used to play together and their parents were young. He heaved a sigh for lost youth.

By now the children were making their way outside to play, along with their cousins, the children of 'young' Jane and her husband Charles..

"Don't you get those clothes dirty," called Charlotte. "Lottie, you be in charge and make sure they don't."

It had taken her many hours and staying up most of the night to make the funeral clothes for them all when James Morehouse had died. She had even enlisted the help of her father Thomas and his treadle machine. After the funeral she had carefully put the clothes away but did not expect them to have to be used quite so soon. Fortunately she had made them plenty big enough so only little Freddy had to have a new outfit made.

The rest of the family spent the afternoon talking about old times until it was time to go. There was much to do. Old James had decreed that his wife would be looked after but he had made a Will to dispose of the assets when she had gone, perhaps little realising that she would pass away so soon after him. Nobody knew exactly what would happen but it was left to the solicitor to sort out and that would take a few weeks. In the meantime Francis still had his job as a Piano Tuner to go back to in Scotland and Frederick had a Lodging House to help run as well as his occasional visit to help Wilfred with his Tea Agent's work.

Charlotte knew she would miss Andria. It had been fun exchanging gossip and making mischief when they knew their blind husbands could not see them.

"You should get a photograph taken of you all" said Andria as they departed. It is possible for ordinary people like us to get their pictures taken now. It is wonderful to have a likeness of ourselves to pass on to our children."

"What a marvellous thing it is!" agreed Charlotte who had only ever seen a photo in the newspaper. It was one of Prince George with his new wife. She still thought that Frederick looked like the second in line to the throne.

"Don't you think Frederick looks like Prince George" Charlotte whispered.

"Yes, he does a bit" laughed Andria. "I don't know who my Frank looks like."

Charlotte looked across at Francis who had a very large belly and grinned.

"Prince Edward I think" she giggled.

What had started as a miserable day ended in laughter as the children were gathered together and they all said their goodbyes before getting the train back to Eastbourne.

For the children, the train journey was an adventure in itself and their spirits were starting to lift. Francis and Andria would be going back to stay a little longer with Jane and Henry before their exceedingly long journey to Scotland. There wasn't very far to go just now though as the couple only lived one street away.

"You take good care of yourselves," shouted Jane as she gathered her two children together. "Come on you two, we have to take Aunt Andria and Uncle Frank back home for a little while longer."

"Don't forget now" called Andria, "get a photograph done and post it to me and then I'll see if he really does look like Prince George."

"And you do one for me" said Charlotte, and I'll look for a photo of Prince Edward. "

"What's that all about?" said Frederick as they parted company and headed for the train station.

"Oh nothing my dear, nothing, nothing for you to worry your pretty little head about," she giggled, gently mimicking the patronising way of some men in Victorian England. The saddest of days ended in laughter.

Prince George

It was a long and wearing journey back to Eastbourne with tired children and both Charlotte and Frederick were glad to be back to normal. Apart from anything else they were losing money as they had not taken on any lodgers recently. It was pointless taking any in when they had no staff and the whole family were away. They were certainly having to watch their pennies and any inheritance from James Morehouse Gosley would be very handy indeed. Even so, Charlotte was determined to find out more about having a photograph taken. It didn't take long. Her wish was granted when she saw an advertisement in the newspaper. *'Come and have your image taken and have something to keep for life. 1/6d'*

"One and sixpence!" cried Frederick. "We can't afford one and sixpence just for a whim!"

"It's not a whim Frederick. I think it is very important to have our image to pass on to our children. Wouldn't you have liked to have had a photograph of your parents to keep? We have nothing of them."

"It would be all right if I could see it," grumbled Frederick, "Besides I will always have a picture of them in my heart."

He could see her point though. It was a marvellous invention. The very idea that your image could be transferred to a piece of paper was just incomprehensible but Andria had been right – it was a new thing that was fast becoming popular, and not just for the newspapers.

He remembered how marvellous it was to see an actual picture in the paper instead of a drawing. Just because he couldn't see he could not deny others.

"We can wear what I made for us all to go to the funeral," went on Charlotte. "At least it is new and the children will look smart." She carried on reading the article and found that the photographer was called Robert Jones and he had a photo booth in his rooms near to the Pier.

The Tailor's Daughter ~ 151

"I shall go and call on Mr. Jones" said Charlotte, "and see if he can take a photograph of us all tomorrow."

"Then wife!" interjected Frederick, "we will get back to concentrating on our lodgers!"

The following day, amid a lot of arguments Charlotte insisted on dressing the children in their funeral clothes again.

"I want your picture to send to Aunt Andria" she informed them.

Only Lottie understood what she was talking about.

"How exciting, my friend Martha, in my school, has had her picture taken and teacher says it is going to be all the rage."

Henry and Mary were arguing and it was all Charlotte could do to keep them apart, but eventually, with the help of Frederick who just wanted to get it all over and done with, the family were ready and they took the short walk down to the Pier and the house of Mr. Robert Jones.

He was a very tall and very slim man with a clean shaven face and a mop of unruly blond hair. He was wearing knee breeches and a smock and looked like something from an illustration in one of the great Arthur Conan Doyle books. Charlotte felt secretly glad that Frederick could not see him for he might have turned round and gone straight out again!

"Come in, come in" he gestured to a small room which was full of what her father would call 'contraptions'. In the middle of the room there was a tripod with a large black cloth draped over it. The children looked on in awe as he beckoned them to some chairs in the corner of the room.

"Now Mr and Mrs Gosley," he smiled, "I suggest you sit at the back with the young lady" – he beckoned to Lottie – "in between you, – got to get you all in the frame don't you see?"

152 ~ *The Tailor's Daughter*

Nobody had a clue what he was talking about but Charlotte guided Frederick to the chair indicated and she sat on the other one with Lottie between them secretly wishing that the photograph had been invented ten years earlier when she had a slimmer waist and her mass of long hair. Those days were long gone.

"Now, you two young men and you little girl, you go in the front." He ushered them to go to where he had in mind but Mary obscured Frederick's face.

"Have to have you sitting down too methinks!" said Robert "and the little one, look we have a little chair for you." Then he turned to Henry. "You, young man, can stand at the side like the big boy that you are."

He stood back to admire his handiwork.

"Now you must not move." He said.

It was a tall order, especially for little Frederick and everyone was feeling just a bit tired. "This had better be good," muttered their father.

"Please don't speak sir," said Robert.

Frederick Senior was beginning to feel heartedly sick of the whole procedure but persevered for the sake of the peace.

Eventually Robert Jones got everybody as he wanted and then, to the amusement of the children, he disappeared under the big black blanket. Within seconds he emerged again.

"Please don't laugh or smile, otherwise the finished result will be blurred. Please, stock still all of you." Now he was starting to get annoyed and the children thought it best to stop giggling.

Back he went under the blanket and held up a sort of stick with his right hand.

"Watch the birdie" he called.

Nobody knew what birdie or where it was but nobody dared move a muscle. After all this was costing one shilling and sixpence.

Suddenly there was a bang and a flash from the stick that made them jump out of their skin and little Frederick cried.

"Got it!" shouted Robert, "Got it! Come back tomorrow Mrs. Gosley and I'll have it developed for you."

The Gosley family were slowly dragging themselves into the 1900's – a decade that was only a couple of months away and which would bring many changes.

The following day Charlotte paid the one shilling and sixpence and collected the result of Robert Jones's labours. She stared at it, unable to put it down. He had made her two copies, one for herself and one to send to Andria in Scotland Frederick held it up to his one eye that he could see a very small amount out of. It was a lost cause but he got the idea.

"Now I have a photograph the same as Mary!" said Lottie when Charlotte showed it to her. "We do look sad though,"

"No" said Mary, "I think we were just frightened. It was all so strange."

"And I still think he looks like Prince George!" Charlotte said to herself.

Frederick, Lottie, Charlotte
Mary, young Frederick, Henry (1899)

❖ ❖ ❖

The new decade, 1900, arrived amid very inclement weather and Charlotte found herself wishing that she was enjoying the New Zealand summer. There had been a terrific influenza outbreak in London which had killed many and laid many others low and things were not going all that well in the Boer

War. In fact, one way and another, things were very depressing and everyone longed for the summer.

Disappointingly, James had left all his assets which remained after the demise of his wife, which amounted to £820 and twopence, to his only daughter Jane. Frederick was totally shocked.

"What on earth was he thinking of!" he cried "read it again woman – are you sure you are reading it right?"

"Yes Frederick, it says all my possessions to go to my daughter Jane Whaley."

"Didn't he leave anything to any of us?"

"Well I suppose, when you think about it" said Charlotte helpfully, "Jane did stick by him and looked after them both in their old age while you boys were gallivanting around the world, and..." she reminded him, "he did help you and Francis out considerably when you first came back from New Zealand."

Frederick had to agree that this was true but even so it had come as a surprise. Then he laughed ironically.

"Well, he might have left me the twopence!"

Suddenly Charlotte was starting to see the Frederick of old. The Frederick who, ten years ago, had been cocky and self assured. She was beginning to think that James had known exactly what he was doing. For years now, since he had lost his sight, her husband had lost his enthusiasm for anything and even the Lodging House had been losing its appeal, but now there was a sudden change.

"Right that does it!" he grumbled, "I think the old boy was testing us all. He wants us to make a go of it on our own two feet. He always taught us boys to do just that. I expect he felt that Jane was not capable and must rely on a husband. If he is looking down on us Charlotte, I shall show him and we will really make this place pay dividends."

She tactfully ignored Frederick's reference to women not being capable!

"We'll make this into the best Lodging House in Eastbourne. He raised his unseeing eyes to the heavens and clenched his fist.

In fact it turned out that James had left a small amount of money to his boys, enough to be of some use, but the bulk of it certainly went to Jane Whaley. Charlotte was pleased to see the spirit come back into her husband and said a silent 'thank you' to her father-in-law..

"What happens if we don't make a go of it?" said Charlotte. "We are not getting the lodgers that we used to."

"I think we will be all right my dear," said Frederick confidently. "I have every faith in us both and we can certainly start taking in more in the holiday season – more and more people are spending holidays here and the beach is always crowded in the summer."

Charlotte wasn't so sure. It would mean taking on staff who would have to be paid. It was as if he had read her thoughts.

"We won't take on any more staff. I will give up that silly job with Wilfred and I will spend all my time helping you. It is what we have always wanted and that is what we will do. Get a pencil and paper woman and we can make up an advertisement for the newspaper."

Clearly James' idea was that the boys could stand on their own two feet but Jane could not and Frederick was going to prove him right.

Charlotte went across to the other side of the street and for the umpteenth time she looked up at the house they had bought two years ago. She was still marvelling at their boldness.

She grimaced to herself. It could certainly do with a coat of paint.

The house was three stories high, very grand and only a stones throw from the sea front. He followed her and put his arm around her shoulders.

"We will make a go of it, we will Charlotte."

She had not seen him this enthusiastic since he lost his sight and she certainly did not want to throw cold water on his plans, but she had many misgivings. It was an awful lot of work, but still neither of them minded hard work. All they had to do was make it pay. With the invention of the photograph and then the 'what the Butler saw' on the Pier and also the End of the Pier Variety Shows, Eastbourne was becoming very popular in the summer. With the Boer War almost over and the men coming home once more it looked like it all might work out well after all. It had been disappointing and hurtful that James left most of his money to his daughter but, as Charlotte suspected, it did have the effect of firing Frederick with an enthusiasm which she had not seen for a long time.

❖ ❖ ❖

Charlotte had been right. It certainly did turn out to be very hard work, but Frederick was true to his word and did everything possible to make the place a success. He could nip up and down the stairs as surely as he could nip up the rigging of the ships he had served on, and he arranged to have the house painted.

It didn't take long to take in more lodgers. Many were temporary and just down to take the sea air for a week or a fortnight, but there were some more permanent ones including a young couple just starting out on their married life just as Charlotte and Frederick did under the wing of James and Jenny at the Sailors Return in Lyttleton Harbour.

These two were Paul and Dorothy Evans. He worked on one of the booths on the pier and she was a chamber maid in one of the numerous hotels. They were no trouble at all and Charlotte was beginning to think that all her doubts had been groundless. Frederick certainly made himself useful with changing bedding and helping to prepare meals. He even helped with the cleaning although often she had to come behind him because he missed a bit. He never knew it though and it did give him some self esteem.

As 1900 gave way to 1901 it was a time of many changes. Charlotte couldn't keep up with it and marvelled every time she read the newspaper to Frederick.

"Look here Frederick, moving pictures!" she exclaimed. "You can actually go and see moving pictures of people. It says here that somebody has taken moving pictures of soldiers in the Boer War. It's incredible."

"You can see moving pictures on the Pier," said Lottie, "in 'What the Butler Saw!'"

"No dear," Charlotte explained. "That is just a series of photographs all put together and flicked quickly. This is proper moving pictures just as if our photograph had come to life."

"In any case," interjected Frederick, "you shouldn't be looking at 'what the Butler saw!' I have heard it is not suitable for young ladies."

He couldn't help wishing it had all come about before he had lost his sight, but he was used to it now and took it all in his stride even though he did feel slightly miffed at not seeing 'What the Butler Saw.'

They heard the sound of one of the lodgers running upstairs and moving around overhead. All had their own keys and were able to get in through the front door and up the stairs without disturbing the main household on the ground floor. Only the two boys used one of the rooms upstairs so that most of the second floor and all of the third floor was used by paying guests.

Lottie was making the most of her last weeks at home. She was fourteen now and would soon be going into service like her mother before her, although Charlotte often wondered why it was always written in tablets of stone that the boys should have the education and the girls be palmed off into service. She had a great deal of sympathy with the suffragette movement.

"Don't worry my dear" she said to her eldest daughter, "you will probably meet a nice boy in service and settle down one day I am sure the Agency will find you a suitable establishment."

Lottie wasn't entirely convinced but most of the girls in her school were in the same boat. They were all waiting to go into service so it wasn't anything unusual.

In total contrast Frederick was busy on the other side of the room teaching Henry his sums. He didn't need his eyesight for that. He did everything in his head and was very clever at calculations.

"You learn your sums my boy and then you will always be in control of your affairs."

Henry sat with an abacus and pencil and paper and listened to his father.

"Now, how many pennies to a shilling Henry?"

"Twelve father!"

"Good boy, now if you have five shillings how many pennies do you have?"

Henry thought for a while and moved the beads on the abacus.

"Sixty!"

"That's my boy, you will go far my son!"

❖ ❖ ❖

Things began to change in 1901 with the death of Queen Victoria. Nobody had seen the old lady much over the past few years. She had closeted herself at Osborne House on the Isle of Wight and suffered badly with rheumatism, but she was part of the fabric of Great Britain and with her passing was the end of another era.

Moving pictures came into their own and you could go to the cinema and see actual film of her coffin atop the gun carriage in the funeral procession through London. This was usually accompanied by somebody playing mournful music on the piano. She had been the longest reigning monarch in British history, soon to be succeeded by her son Edward, who would only reign for just nine years.

Just for once Charlotte found herself wishing that she still lived in London so that she could have seen the procession at first hand.

For the Gosley family there were also changes. It was now time for fourteen year old Lottie to go to be in service with a well heeled family in another part of Sussex. It couldn't be put off any longer. It meant that they would only see her once a month and young Mary would have the bedroom largely to herself.

The agency had found her a position working for The Maltwood family. At first it would be as a Parlour Maid but also she

The Tailor's Daughter ~ 161

would have some duties looking after the children, Louisa, Percy and Ivy.

For women generally it was the beginning of a whole new era. The tight restraint of Victorian England was relaxing and there was even talk that women might have the vote one day, which Frederick, like most men, thought was totally ridiculous.

"A woman's place is in the home!" he remarked when Charlotte read from the paper to him as she usually did every night.

"That will change one day Frederick" said Charlotte, "you just wait and see – we women have a right to show you men what we can do."

"Poppycock!" laughed Frederick. "It's men's business."

"Just you wait husband. The Suffragette Movement is getting stronger by the day."

"Just trouble makers," retorted Frederick and turned his attention back to his sons.

Meanwhile the boys concentrated on their sums although half their minds were occupied with how to get out to play at the earliest opportunity.

❖ ❖ ❖

13. In Mother's footsteps

(Ten years later 1911)

Charlotte stood on the quayside at Plymouth and watched history repeating itself. She had come, escorted by her brother-in-law Wilfred and young Henry, to see her eldest daughter Lottie, now aged twenty-four, off to Australia. What could she say? What could she do? The child was only copying what her mother did before her at, co-incidentally, exactly the same age. She was a grown woman now but she would always be a child in her mother's eyes. The one saving grace as far as Charlotte was concerned was that she was not doing as she had done, and going all by herself. As it had turned out Lottie's employer Mr. Maltwood had died leaving his wife and three children. It was Louisa Maltwood who decided to emigrate and take her children with her and she had given Lottie the chance to go with them.

"It is such an opportunity!" Lottie had said to her surprised parents on her visit home. "I can go as part of the family as a nurse."

Frederick had been less than pleased but there was little he could as she was now of age "Why the dickens are you choosing Australia when you were born in New Zealand?" snapped Frederick angrily when Lottie had first broached the subject.

"That's precisely why Father," she replied. "I am a New Zealand citizen by birth so I can go there at any time from Australia if I want to."

The Tailor's Daughter ~ 163

He couldn't understand why she could not have got another job if the Maltwoods were emigrating. In fact, she did have many sleepless nights trying to make up her mind whether to go or not, but, just like her mother before her, she had that urge to travel and be her own woman.

The advancement in shipping and the shorter journey was, however, of little comfort just at this precise moment and Charlotte cursed the newspapers for advertising emigration all the time. She could just imagine it – after all it had happened to her – all the newspapers arriving at the Maltwood household and Louisa leaving them strewn around where Lottie could see them and all saying what a better life she would have in Australia or New Zealand. Indeed, even her young brother Thomas, now in his thirties, was hankering after emigrating to Canada! There were even posters plastered on the walls of shops and post offices. There was no getting away from it.

Now the time had come and the older woman hugged her daughter and found herself appreciating what her own mother must have felt like all those years ago when she had come home from her job as a parlour maid in Cambridge and, seemingly out of the blue, calmly announced that she was going on an immigrant ship to New Zealand. She might as well have been saying that she was going to the moon or the stars! However, things had moved on since her day and the ships were bigger and better now. Also the journey would be slightly shorter for Lottie because she was going to New South Wales, Australia via the Suez Canal. This cut the journey time down to forty five days. Fortunately too, she was accompanied by the much older Louisa Maltwood and her three children who looked to be ranging between ten and thirteen. Louisa came over to introduce herself to Charlotte.

"Don't worry" she smiled "we shall look after our Lottie, won't we children?"

There was a chorus of "yes!" from the assembled company and they moved discreetly to one side while Lottie said her goodbyes.

"Father was not very pleased with me was he mother?" she grinned.

"Don't worry Charlotte" the older woman replied as she lapsed back to the name that her daughter was christened with. "I'll take care of him."

Lottie gave her mother a hug.

Charlotte smiled as she thought of her father Thomas when she had first told them of her plans to go to New Zealand.

"Blimey," he had said after coming face to face with yet another poster. "half Britain is going off to the other side of the blinkin' world – there will be none of us left here soon and now even my daughter is going." Little did he know that his granddaughter would be going there as well.

She wondered what he would make of it all and suddenly felt a sadness when she thought of him. Thomas died just three years ago and her mother, now an old lady, had decided to move back to live with Minnie in London. He had left her all his sewing equipment including his precious new Singer treadle machine which she was already making good use of. In fact, some of her handiwork was even now on its way to Australia on the back of Lottie. Bless him – she wondered again what he would say about history repeating itself like this.

What was it that Mrs. Catchpole had once said when she was in service at the Brownlow's? "If God had meant us to go to the other side of the world he would have given us wings."

The Tailor's Daughter ~ 165

But nobody could blame anyone for wanting to better themselves. Both Victorian and Edwardian England could be very harsh to those who were not born with silver spoons in their mouths and the writings of Dickens were very accurate, especially in the East End of London. These new emerging countries in the Commonwealth seemed to have so much to offer for young people. After all, there was no doubt at all that if Frederick had not lost his eyesight they would have stayed out there and would have made a life for the children in the lovely modern town of Wellington with its backdrop of mountains.

❖ ❖ ❖

She felt a little pang of jealousy as Lottie approached her to give her a final hug before joining her employer and embarking and wished that she could put back the clock a few years.

Frederick had not come to see her off. It was too far and he had said his goodbyes at the Railway Station. Despite assurances to the contrary from his wife he still felt guilty that they were forced to come home and it had all been to no avail. Going to see his daughter disappear for 'God knows how long' on a ship he could not see was just rubbing salt into the wound, so he was eternally grateful to Wilfred who had, once again, come to the rescue and offered to escort Charlotte on the train.

"I don't know why" grumbled young Henry who was full of his own self importance. "I am perfectly capable of looking after my mother."

"You are still a lad," Frederick had argued. "It would probably end up with your mother escorting you. As for Lottie, she will have enough on her mind and will be with her employers. I'll be happier with a grown man to accompany your mother but you can go with them if you wish."

With the wind taken out of his sails Henry had accepted his father's wishes – though he failed to understand why he was so fussy when mother had gone all the way to New Zealand by herself back in the eighteen eighties. Surely they didn't need Wilfred just to go from Eastbourne to Plymouth! As it turned out though his uncle had been a godsend in managing his way around the train stations and the harbour and fighting through the crowds of people.

Now they were together on the quayside watching Lottie and the Maltwood family go aboard the SS Tahiti. Indeed, the crew were hurrying people along because the ship was ready to leave.

"Goodbye Uncle Wilfred" said Lottie, and tears filled her eyes despite herself.

She turned to Henry and gave him a big hug and kiss which he immediately wiped away. At his age he didn't go in for being kissed by his sister in public. Nevertheless, he put his arms round her fully aware that it may be some considerable time before he ever saw her again.

Lottie saved her last hug for her mother and Charlotte could contain herself no longer and the tears streamed down her face. She had never imagined in a million years that now, in 1911 she would be going through the exact same procedure as her own mother did in 1884. It was a lifetime ago and yet, in many ways, like yesterday.

"Don't worry Mother, I will be fine." The women hugged each other again. "I'll write as soon as I can and don't forget I have been with this family for ten years. I will be well looked after, I am quite sure of that."

"I would not be allowing you to go if I didn't think as much" Charlotte replied, knowing perfectly well that Lottie was as

The Tailor's Daughter ~ 167

headstrong as she was at the same age and no amount of persuasion would have served to stop her.

Lottie ran off to join the family and the rest of the crowds milling towards the great liner, just as a band began to strike up on the quayside and people threw streamers into the air.

"Just look at the size of that ship!" remarked Wilfred. "Can you believe the size of that?"

It was indeed huge and at least twice the size of the 'British King' which Charlotte had travelled on to New Zealand. Things had certainly moved on apace and she felt comforted at the sheer enormity of it. Not for Lottie the tossing about around the Cape of Good Hope and the vessel relying on sail for most of this way. Not for her being slung from side to side in unbelievable gales and being thoroughly sick in the process. Well at least, possibly not quite as much anyway although it was inevitable that they would get their fair share of rough seas.

"I read that it is over seven thousand tons" said Henry. Charlotte grinned to herself. Trust Henry to know that. However, if the boy was right then the SS Tahiti left the three thousand five hundred ton 'British King' way behind, and at the time she had felt that was enormous. It certainly seemed so when you walked around it.

She looked along the length of the quayside at this huge vessel and wondered how on earth they stayed afloat. It was also high and just like looking up at one of the huge four story buildings that were being built these days.

She wondered what Jenny and James Braithwaite would make of this great big thing if it were to come into Lyttleton Harbour and, goodness only knew, they had been used to some mighty ships, some carrying as many as five hundred souls, but never anything like this monster.

She watched Lottie climb the gangway. She was dressed in bright purple and had a jaunty hat on her head. Since the death of Victoria the fashions were becoming more relaxed and some women were even starting to show a bit of ankle. Lottie hadn't gone that far, but gone were the tight corsets and stays that Charlotte had been used to at the same age.

The band continued to play and there was much cheering and more streamers thrown as the gangplanks were pulled aboard and the mighty engines started to thud. Charlotte watched Lottie until she disappeared in the crowd but suddenly there was a cry and she looked up. She could just about make out her daughter's dark head and her arm waving the purple hat in the air like a flag. She was leaning over the rail on the third deck and waving along with the other passengers. More tears started to flow down Charlotte's cheeks.

"Oh shut up you silly woman!" she said to herself out loud.

She felt her son's hand take hers and Wilfred's arm go around her shoulders.

"Don't worry" said Wilfred, "she has to have her adventures just as you did and I am sure she will be back one day."

"Ships are getting faster and bigger" volunteered Henry "the journey will become easier."

After what seemed like an age the moorings were set free and there was a change in the tone of the engines as the great vessel edged its way from the quayside. Charlotte looked along Plymouth Sound to the direction of the open sea and spotted the pilot ship lying in wait. Suddenly she thought of her father-in-law, old James Morehouse Gosley – he had been gone over ten years now – and the years he had spent doing just that very job out of Deal and around the Kent coast. He had been such a nice old boy, although it still grated that he had favoured his

The Tailor's Daughter ~ 169

daughter so much. Then she thought of Frederick's new found sparkle and determination and once again told herself that her father-in-law knew what he was doing.

All the passengers lined the decks and now she had lost sight of Lottie. She remembered what it was like and knew that it would be mayhem as everyone pushed and shoved to get their last look of the coast as the band played on and on. It was the 18th October 1911.

Little did anyone know, as the crowds watched the huge ship glide towards open sea, that Wilfred's words about coming back would come true in just three years time, and for a reason that nobody could have imagined in a million years

❖ ❖ ❖

The house seemed empty now that Lottie had gone. True they were used to not seeing her much but that was expected with her being in service. Up until now her bed had always been there for her and all her clothes and possessions filled up half the cupboards. Now Mary had the room to herself and even she was barely there any more as she was off in service herself working as a parlour maid in nearby Hastings. Only the boys remained at home as Frederick was at school and Henry was training to be a teacher.

Charlotte couldn't help but continue to think how unfair it was that girls had to go out into service at the age of fourteen and yet the boys could continue their studies. Frederick didn't think it was unfair at all.

"After all my dear, it is the boys who have to be the bread winners and not the girls."

"Really my dear?" replied Charlotte a little sarcastically, "well how come that just at the moment it is our girls who are earning a living and the boys who are not?"

"Frederick and Henry will one day though" argued Henry "they will never be poor if they can do sums – why, Henry does all the accounts for me now."

Charlotte realised that it was pointless to argue the toss any more, but she secretly hoped that the Suffragette movement had some success. There had been talk that women would get the vote one day, but that 'one day' seemed a long way off at the moment. It was singularly unfair.

She picked up the newspaper and settled down to read some of the articles to Frederick.

"Goodness me Frederick!" she exclaimed "there is a drawing here of a ship they are building in Belfast and it is huge!" She scanned through the text twice because she could not believe what she was reading the first time. "Oh that is just ridiculous, just ridiculous I say."

"For goodness sake what are you talking about woman!" snapped Frederick. The frustration at not being able to pick up the newspaper and read for himself was getting to be just too much. He vowed that as soon as possible he would get one of the wireless things that everyone was talking about.

"It says here they are building the biggest ship ever to be built – ever – in the world. It is to be forty-six thousand tons or more. Forty-six *thousand* tons. I thought Lottie's ship was big enough but this is just unbelievable."

"I'll bet it is a joke" laughed Frederick, "you would not get a ship of that size afloat." He thought for a minute. "Why, for goodness sake, the British King was three thousand tons and that was big enough when I used to walk around it on watch."

The Tailor's Daughter

"It says here it is going to be like a floating city and that it will carry over two thousand passengers. It's going to be called the Titanic."

"Who on earth would build a thing like that?" laughed Frederick.

"It says here that work has started on it and it is being built by Harland and Wolff in Belfast."

"I might have known," said Frederick "trust the Irish to be barmy."

"Frederick – they have a drawing of it here and it is standing on its end to show that if it *were* on its end it would be the height of the Eiffel Tower. That gives you the idea of how long it is."

Neither of them had ever seen the Eiffel Tower in real life but they had seen plenty of images of it and knew how tall it was in comparison with other buildings in the picture.

"They think it is going to be ready for launch next year, in 1912."

"Well I'll believe it when it happens," sneered Frederick, "that can't be possible."

"They reckon it will be unsinkable."

"Huh!" said Frederick. He had other things to think about, such as what were they going to do when their tenancy came to an end.

He didn't know where the time had gone but the ten years were soon to be completed and then the tenancy would not be renewed. They had just about managed to make the Lodging House pay its way, but sometimes rooms were empty, especially in the winter. Besides, the owners had made it clear that they had the property earmarked for some other use.

"Money talks" said Frederick, when it became clear that it would not be renewed. "They can make much more money if they turn the place into a hotel or offices."

Charlotte carefully folded the newspaper up. She would show the article about the Titanic to Henry. It would be just the sort of thing that would interest him.

Frederick lay back in the chair and closed his eyes.

"Forty six thousand tons," he muttered. "Ridiculous!"

To be honest, Charlotte wasn't all that concerned about the end of the tenancy looming large. Frederick was beginning to lose interest again and, although he worked hard to make the Lodging House pay and did many of the jobs that a sighted person would do, they were getting older and had to think of their future. As for herself, she had a hankering to get back to tailoring again. She had inherited all her father's equipment and 'know how' and people always needed to be clothed. Admittedly many people were buying ready made stuff which sometimes came in from abroad, but there was always work for a good dressmaker and tailor. Between what she could earn in this capacity and what they had made over the past ten years with running the lodging house it would be possible to buy a small semi detached house but it was Frederick who was the worry. He was still only fifty seven and not the sort of man to want to just sit idly by and watch his wife working. It was against all his principles.

It was difficult to ignore Frederick when he was in one of his moods. The new spirit he had found when his father died and left most of his money to his sister had worn off and he still missed his life in the Merchant Navy. He stalked around the house like a wounded tiger and quite frequently found solace down at the sea front. That was where he could listen to the seagulls and the roar of the ocean together with all the sounds of activity on the pier. In fact, if ever Frederick went missing Charlotte always knew where to find him. He would be either sitting on the sea wall or talking to the man who ran the Punch and Judy show and some of the other attractions, such as the very popular 'What the Butler Saw' machines.

Both Charlotte and Frederick knew that they could not put off the inevitable for much longer. They were not even getting the tenants any more. People were venturing farther afield for their holidays and it was quite common for the whole of the third floor upstairs to be empty.

"The sooner we move from here the better," said Frederick one day when he came down from helping Charlotte change the upstairs sheets. "We only have Arthur and Betty Tyler this week."

Arthur and Betty were a 'double act' who worked in the end of the Pier Show. Arthur sang and Betty danced. They were in the back room on the second floor, but kept themselves to themselves. They always turned up at eight o'clock for breakfast and then were never seen again until they finished their performances and came in for the night. They were no trouble and paid their rent on time. They had clearly been around for a while doing the music halls and were used to their nomadic way of life. Frederick would be sorry when the time came to ask them to leave but they would have to find somewhere else and that was that.

He sometimes wished that he had a good voice and then maybe he could earn some money in the same way, but that wasn't to be. He would think of something though and in the meantime he would get Charlotte onto the job of scanning the papers for suitable properties to move to which they could afford with what they had saved during the past ten years. That would be her job. His job would be to find a way of earning a living.

They received their first letter from Lottie some three months after she had left. It was a very long letter full of the detail of her journey and what she had been up to since arriving in Australia.

"Come on woman" cried Frederick impatiently, "read it out, read it out!"

"It's postmarked Coogee in New South Wales," said Charlotte as she popped her glasses on the end of her nose.

"Never mind where it is postmarked, what has she been up to? Is she safe?"

Charlotte started to read...

"I've met a lovely man called Percy Neale and I think we might get married one day...."

"Damn it!" exclaimed Frederick, "whatever is she thinking of, she hasn't been there five minutes."

Charlotte threw her head back and laughed.

"Now I know how our parents felt!" she giggled. "Don't worry husband, I'm sure our daughter has found somebody worthy of her." She carried on reading...

> "We have settled down out here but I am not being nursemaid to the children any more. I have a job as a dressmaker although for the time being I am still lodging with Louisa Maltwood. I am trying to use all the skills you taught me mother. I see Percy every day. He is from England but of course we will marry here. Then the plan is to go north to Queensland and then possibly end up in New Zealand to have a family."

The Tailor's Daughter ~ 175

"Humph! She has it all worked out doesn't she." grunted Frederick.

"She is a big girl now," replied Charlotte, a little unnecessarily and she does not want to be in service for ever."

They were interrupted by the sound of the boys coming in from school and, in Henry's case, accounting college, and Charlotte decided she had best get some tea on the table.

❖ ❖ ❖

It took nearly a year before they found a nice little terrace house in Winter Road, Eastbourne. With just three bedrooms it was much easier to manage both from the point of view of finances and also of work. Also the boys were starting to bring in some money now, especially Henry who was not only a trainee teacher but earned money with his accounting. Charlotte was also able to run a fairly successful business with her tailoring and dressmaking. They also had the small amount of money they had inherited and invested from James Gosley. Nevertheless Charlotte was quite sorry to leave Marine Road and for a while she did miss the hustle and bustle of all the paying guests.

❖ ❖ ❖

Now that there was less work to do, Frederick spent more of his time down at the seafront. He tried to help as much as he could in the house but he really needed to do something for himself.

He had done quite well working as a Tea Agent but modern equipment was coming in and, try as he might, his brother-in-law could not find enough for him to do. It was hard times and everyone was struggling for a crust.

He could hear the sound of the seagulls and the people chattering as they ventured onto the pier in the spring sunshine when suddenly he felt a slap on his back.

"Hello Frederick old boy!" he knew the voice straight away and looked up to see the outline of Arthur Tyler.

"Hello Arthur, back for another season?"

"Yes if they will have us – we still have to earn a crust don't you know."

Suddenly another sound filled the air. It was that of the nearby street organ.

"There you are, that would do for you!" laughed Arthur. "Old Harry there has been saying for months that he would like someone to take over from him."

Frederick laughed but it gave him food for thought as Arthur walked away to join his wife who was busy looking at hats in a nearby shop window. It was something he could do. After all, how difficult would it be to turn the handle? The owner would collect the takings and he would just get a fee. Moreover it meant that he could stop outside and get the sea air. The idea appealed to him.

He hauled himself up from where he had been perched on the sea wall and grimaced as his body ached. If this was old age he wasn't very keen on it.

"I hear you are looking for somebody to take over from you Harry?" he cried when he got within earshot.

"Not 'arf" moaned Harry. "I'm much too old to stand here all day and I have had enough of it." He thought for a minute. "Do you want a job Freddy? No strings attached, I'll give you a set fee and I'll just sit about and watch the takings drop into the box."

Well that answered one question for Frederick. The one of how was he going to keep his eye on the money with his impaired vision? Most people were honest but there were also plenty of rogues who would steal from a blind man.

"Well provided you look after the money I don't mind turning the handle!" giggled Frederick. "Mind you, I do not know what the missus will say."

He could just about make out the shape of the thing. It was quite large and could be wheeled along the road. The music was played by means of a large drum which turned as you moved the handle. Harry gave him a demonstration.

"See just a steady turn – not too quick or you will have people marching down the road in double time." He rubbed his arm, "it's all too much for the old rheumatism for me Freddy."

Frederick turned the handle and a loud chorus of "My old man said follow the band" came out of it.

"Ha ha," he laughed, "a little bit of Marie Lloyd eh."

"There is just one more thing" said Harry. "You only live round the corner in Winter Road, and I can no longer keep it in my little flat that I have just moved to. I should need you to take it home with you each afternoon when you finish playing."

Frederick wondered again what Charlotte would have to say about it, but he knew she would be glad of the money.

And so it was that at the end of that eventful year of 1911 Frederick Gosley could be seen walking down Winter Road pushing the street organ like some elaborate baby carriage. He was met at the doorstep by Henry and young Frederick. Both the boys looked a little bit the worse for wear for alcohol. Frederick thought they were enjoying it just a bit too much lately and young Frederick was definitely a bad influence on Henry. He had plans for his eldest son and hoped that one day he would qualify to become a Maths teacher. The younger lad was a different matter and there were times when Frederick and

Charlotte wondered just what they were going to do about him. He certainly was not going to be an academic but he did seem to be very interested in the new fangled cars that were filling the streets. Maybe he would become a mechanic, but not if he spent every day boozing in the local hostelry.

"Father, what the devil have you got there?" It was young Frederick that first spoke.

"A means of earning a living my lad – something that you ought to be doing instead of boozing down at the Black Swan." The two boys rolled around laughing.

"Come on, lets have a go!" cried Henry. "Come on Father, be a sport."

"No, it is only to be used on the beach. I don't want to lose my job before I have done anything."

He paused for a minute to catch his breath after pushing the thing up the hill. "It's locked anyway."

Henry and young Frederick helped him to get into the house and he braced himself for the wrath of Charlotte.

He was not to be disappointed. Charlotte had seen him coming up the road and was waiting in the parlour for him, her hands on her hips, her greying hair flicked with flour from her baking.

"What in the name of all that is holy have you got there Frederick?" she gasped. "Are you expecting me to keep that thing in my front parlour?"

Suddenly to Frederick it looked bigger in the little house than it did on the seafront. The boys ran away laughing leaving their parents to sort our Frederick's latest venture.

"It's my way of earning a living Charlotte." He pushed into the room and stood back and admired it. "You have to admit that it makes a nice piece of furniture."

"No it does not" cried his harassed wife, "and look at the wheels all over my nice clean lino. It is not coming in here, you can keep it out in the porch."

And so it was, and after much argument, that Frederick became a street organ player in Eastbourne.

❖ ❖ ❖

As far as Charlotte was concerned she would put up with it in the interests of Frederick earning some money. Most of her time she got away from the men by visiting her friend Susannah Mann and her daughters Margaret and Constance who lived in nearby Commercial Road.

"Oh, I am fed up with being in a house of men." She told Susannah. "I'd rather be here doing my sewing in peace with you and leave them to get on with it."

Susannah gave her a knowing look.

"You don't need to give me one of your looks" laughed Charlotte, "don't worry, I still love the old devil, but since he got that barrel organ the place is not my own. He does earn a bit from it but really I am the bread winner in our house and he has accepted that."

"Well it is different anyway," laughed Margaret as she put the finishing touches to a fancy waistcoat. "Does he do the chores though, that's what I would like to know. There are not many men who would do housework."

"Oh Frederick will, he does the housework sometimes." She thought for a little while. "Mind you he is not very good at it."

The four women laughed together. In truth Charlotte was quite contented with her lot and as for the old street organ, well, she had got used to it now. It was part of the furniture.

She had done very well since her father died and left her all his sewing and tailoring equipment so she was able to make a good living. She couldn't help but think that her parents would have been very proud at how things had turned out. She was a very strong woman and she had a secret admiration of the likes of Emily Pankhurst who was causing mayhem in London in her quest for the vote for women. Indeed, at times she wasn't very secretive about it at all, especially when she was in the company of her husband and two sons, all three of whom were 'typical men'.

"Oh mother, it's ridiculous that women should get the vote," said Henry one morning when they were discussing yet another antic by Mrs. Pankhurst. "The woman is just a trouble maker."

"I agree," muttered young Freddy who was busy getting ready to go and meet a young lady. "There are much more important things to think about than women getting the vote."

The Tailor's Daughter ~ 181

Charlotte had to laugh to herself. She had crossed oceans to reach New Zealand all by herself, had run a lodging house and now had a successful Drapery business which she could run from home or, if she wanted some female company, at Commercial Road with Susannah. Yet there were these three men in her life decrying votes for women! It was inconceivable. She surveyed her two sons. They were young men now and Henry especially had filled out and had the stocky appearance of her side of the family. He bore a remarkable resemblance to the young Winston Churchill who had made such a name for himself in the Army and now in politics. It was very rare that you could lift a newspaper without seeing a picture of him, usually looking very smart in his Army uniform. The whole family admired the man, especially Henry who was very influenced by him. However, it still came as a surprise when Henry suddenly announced one day that he intended to join the Army!

Charlotte had just put a large side of beef into the kitchen range to cook for later on that day in order to feed the young men. Frederick was tinkering with the new fangled wireless and trying to listen to the latest news about the forthcoming launch of the huge great ship the Titanic. However, Henry suddenly had their undivided attention.

"I think I will join the Army," he announced, "I am sure they must need people who can do sums as well as people to go out and shoot."

Frederick felt torn between thinking that it would do the boy some good and, at the same time, thinking that the child was deluding himself and what a waste of all that education.

"What are you talking about boy" he laughed "you are supposed to be training to be a teacher. There are wars going on everywhere. Why, it is not that long ago since that Churchill fella that you so admire came back from fighting the Boers."

"I know father, I have studied him. He has also been in the Sudan and India. It must have been really exciting."

"Besides" said Frederick grumpily, "you talk about the Army. What is wrong with the Navy or going to sea? We are seafarers in our family, not Army!"

Charlotte thought of all the dead and hoped fervently that her son would change his mind.

"Don't worry mother," he assured her when he saw the look on her face, "I'll wait until I have passed my exams but I really need to do something with my life."

"But why the bloody Army?" said Frederick again.

"I just don't think I would enjoy going to sea Father" replied Henry, "and I do admire Churchill. I would like to be like him."

Charlotte kept quiet. Well how could they say anything really? Both she and Frederick had gone right over to the other side of the world and into a country which, at the time, most people knew very little about. Now her children were fleeing the nest. She could understand Frederick being miffed that Henry would be the first Gosley not to go to sea though. She knew, because she had seen their graves in the churchyard at Deal, that seafaring Gosleys could be traced back to as far as the seventeen hundreds. But times change and both she and Frederick would have to accept it.

No more was said about Henry joining the Army for another few months. Instead, quite suddenly all the talk was of the great ship, The Titanic and its launch from Belfast and it's visit to Southampton before it's maiden voyage across the Atlantic.

"Absolutely crackers!" said Frederick for the hundredth time that year. "Fancy building a ship that size." He listened carefully to the report of the launching on the wireless. Not that anybody else could hear it as he had to listen with earphones to the crackling commentary coming across the airwaves. Charlotte still found the whole business most perplexing but it was hard to find a newspaper these days because every time she put one down so either Henry or young Freddy picked it up.

There was a visit from her brother-in-law Wilfred and it was all he could talk about, and he fully intended to drive to Southampton to see the great ship.

"I'll take the two lads if you like Charlotte," he told her. "We can all go in my motor car."

Charlotte, like her father before her, thought that the motor car was just a 'contraption' but there was nothing she could say to put them off. She knew that times were changing fast and the motor car was here to stay. She secretly would have liked to have gone to see the Titanic herself but thought better of it. She knew Frederick would not be able to see much and, in any case, with Wilfred taking the boys out of her hair for a while it gave a couple of days of peace and quiet so that she could finish of a suit she was making. She also had some letters to write to Australia. Lottie was still in New South Wales and her romance with Percy was really blossoming with real talk of marriage.

> "I'm still earning a living with my sewing and tailoring" she wrote, "and Percy hopes to take me up to Queensland next year. I miss you all but I do feel as though this is where I belong, with Percy."

Charlotte was able to write back to Lottie all about the Titanic and about her father playing the street organ on Eastbourne seafront.

"I'll bet that will amuse her!" she said out loud.

"What was that dear?" said Frederick.

"Oh nothing dear, nothing." She smiled. "You get back to your wireless."

Their peace was shattered when the boys returned and they could talk about nothing else but this great big ship.

"Mother, you should have seen it," cried an excited Henry. "It was bigger than a street of houses in London, and so high up."

"Well it beats me how it floats," said young Frederick. "It carries about two thousand passengers and they told us there is almost as much depth below the waterline as there is above."

"And the bands were playing and it was so exciting," laughed Henry. "Oh how I wish I could have joined them on that huge great ship."

"It's the biggest ship ever built," he went on, "it's like a floating city."

"Damned silly if you ask me" came a voice from a disgruntled Frederick. He was busy polishing his street organ ready for the day and was fed up with hearing about the daft ship. "No good will come of it, you mark my words. "Besides" he grunted "I thought you were adverse to the sea Henry?"

"I don't think you would know you were on the sea in that thing." Henry replied.

Frederick did not want to be proved right in his fears about this goliath of a ship. He really didn't and it gave him no satisfaction at all when the news started to come in that it had sunk in the Atlantic. First it was rumours – somebody had heard it from somebody else and the people who normally danced around the street organ became more subdued. Then the rumours started to have more substance to them. It was the 16th April 1912.

By the time Frederick got home the town was buzzing with the news and then finally he heard it for himself on his crackling radio. He had the earphones on and didn't hear Charlotte as she came into the room from the shops. His face was ashen as the enormity of the sinking started to hit home.

"Husband you look as though you have seen a ghost," said Charlotte as she removed her hat and coat. "are they still talking about that big ship? I heard it had sunk. I thought it was unsinkable."

He removed his earphones and looked with shocked face at his wife.

"Charlotte, it has gone down with the loss of one thousand five hundred souls."

Neither of them could speak for a minute. It was Frederick that broke the silence.

"Seems it hit an iceberg, They are still trying to find survivors but there won't be any – not in those seas."

The sinking of the Titanic was in the forefront of people's minds for months and years afterwards, especially for Henry and young Freddy who had seen the great ship first hand and knew exactly what it looked like and what a huge loss it was.

"One thousand five hundred souls" said Henry to himself. "One thousand five hundred souls. It doesn't bear thinking about."

"But it was supposed to be unsinkable," said Charlotte again.

❖ ❖ ❖

14. (1913) "The War to end all Wars"

If Charlotte and Frederick thought that Henry's desire to join the Army would go away then they were mistaken. The talk everywhere was still of the sinking of the Titanic, when, at the end of 1913, and with rumblings of war in Europe, he finally announced that he was going to join the Royal Army Service Corps. He had passed his accounting exams and he felt that he now might be qualified to work in the accounts and yet still, maybe, travel abroad and see some sights. After all, other members of the Gosley family had done so – why not him?

"Actually father" he said when Frederick told him he was mad, "I'm not as mad as you think. There is talk of conscription and at least this way I will get to choose what I do instead of the Army sending me to the Infantry."

Frederick had to concede that his son was not as daft as he thought he was!

As far as Charlotte was concerned it was her young boy who left the house one summer morning to go for his recruit training but a man came back after six months, and he looked resplendent in his new uniform. Not for the first time, his mother marvelled at how much he looked like the young Winston Churchill.

"My, let me look at you!" she cried. "Oh Frederick, see how smart he is."

Frederick came up close to Henry and tried to see him out of his one half good eye. It was enough to see that his son was quite grown up.

The Tailor's Daughter ~ 187

"I wish that other little upstart Freddy would have joined," he grumbled. "He could do with a Sergeant Major behind him."

Winston Churchill

Henry Gosley

But the rumblings of war would not go away and with the assassination of the Archduke Franz Ferdinand in June of 1914 the devastation that was to engulf Europe and the Middle East seemed inevitable. By August Britain had declared war on Germany and the whole nation was in despair, Charlotte and Frederick included.

For the time being Henry would be stationed at the Inkerman Barracks which was not far from Woking in Surrey, but everybody knew that it was only a matter of time before he would have to go abroad. However, he had been right. At least he had been able to choose the Regiment he would be in and had been able to avoid going in the Infantry. He wanted to travel but maybe not under these circumstances and nobody knew what lay in store.

Far away in Australia, young Lottie and her Percy married at last. This good news which had taken three months to reach Britain was closely followed by another letter saying that she had just had their first baby, a little girl who they called Louise Frances. Charlotte had just got used to that bit of news when a further letter arrived which was yet another bombshell in an already shell shocked household.

> *"We are coming home for a while Mother. Percy has felt it to be his duty to go and fight on the side of the British. He has volunteered and is going to drive mules for the Army. I'm desolated but so proud of him."*

It was with total mixed feelings that Charlotte read the letter out to Frederick. On the one hand she was thrilled that the family were coming home and she would have a chance to see her grandchild, but horrified at the idea of her son-in-law looking after mules in the trenches! What was he thinking about?

Already there were stories reaching Britain about the Somme and Ypres and the number of lives lost there. There were even pictures in the paper of the utter complete annihilation of vast areas with trees blown apart and buildings flattened to the ground.

She went round to see Susannah and the girls but the atmosphere was subdued, and the tailoring work was beginning to tail off as well. So many men were going to the front so less orders coming in for any of the ladies. She could not get her mind off

Lottie, Percy and baby Louise, not to mention what might befall Henry. The whole thing was too frightening for words.

"Have you seen in the shops lately?" moaned Margaret. "Most of the shelves are empty and they say stuff is going to be rationed soon."

"I don't mind going without just as long as the men come back", said Constance as the tears welled up in her eyes. "My William has gone and I don't know when I shall ever see him again."

Charlotte knew this. Men from all over the country were leaving their loved ones and answering the call to arms. So many men were being lost and soon there would be conscription. It wasn't just in Europe either. Many men were fighting the Turks in some far off place called The Dardanelles and Gallipoli and many were kept in captivity. All sorts of horrible stories about their treatment were circulating and about how they had to do forced marches across the desert until they collapsed and were left for dead. It all seemed like a nightmare that they could not wake up from.

The girls carried on with their sewing in silence but suddenly there was an almighty thud which sounded as though it was right out to sea and yet loud enough to rattle the cups on the dresser.

"Oh my good gawd, what was that?" gasped Charlotte, immediately forgetting her decorum and lapsing straight back into her cockney accent.

"Those are the bombs in the tunnels along the Western front," said Constance. "William's father told me that the British have been making huge tunnels under the ground and planting explosives. The sound is so loud that we can hear them over here on the coast. There is a story that it was heard in Downing Street when the cabinet were having a meeting."

"I heard" added Susannah, "that old Elsie Robbins has four sons that have gone away to fight."

"Oh its just too terrible for words!" said Charlotte.

By now Constance had dissolved into uncontrollable tears and they thought it would be prudent to drop the conversation and try and do a bit of sewing. Susannah made some tea.

Taking into account the length of time that mail took to get to Britain from Australia Charlotte guessed that it would not be long before they got a cable saying that Lottie and Percy had arrived. Even that was fraught with danger and she did wonder at the sense of putting themselves at so much risk just so that Percy could go and drive mules! After all, the war was at sea as well as on land and the passenger ships had to run the gauntlet of torpedoes and submarines, as well as the vast German warships. Much as she wanted to see Lottie and her new grand-daughter, she did think they were slightly mad.

The family arrived home early in 1915 by which time the new baby was one year old and Lottie already pregnant again.

"Oh Mother, you have no idea" said Lottie. "We were in such danger and the ship had to make a huge detour right out into the Atlantic and back again in order to avoid the German Warships in the Channel."

Frederick cuddled baby Louise and just kept his mouth shut. He too thought they were both completely mad but he did secretly admire Percy for his devotion to duty and his allegiance to the crown.

Percy Neale stayed just one night before reporting for duty at the Aldershot Barracks up in Hampshire. He had already volunteered whilst in Australia so it was all just a formality. Both

Charlotte and Lottie were in floods of tears but it fell on deaf ears.

"I'm committed now," he told them. "If I don't go now I will be classed as a deserter." There were more tears and they all stood and waved to him as he walked down the road to the train station.

❖ ❖ ❖

"Well it has certainly been hectic in this household lately," laughed Charlotte as she watched the antics of the little baby blowing bubbles at Frederick. She was a dear little thing with a mop of dark brown hair just like Lottie and Mary were born with. She brushed her hand over her own ruefully. Hers was completely grey now and yet it didn't seem like five minutes ago that she too arrived home from the other side of the world with a new baby girl. She had also had a decent figure then, not that she had ever been slim, but her waistline had expanded even more over the years. Her thoughts were interrupted by the arrival of Henry home on leave for a day and, moreover he had a girlfriend with him.

Charlotte was quite taken aback. Henry had plenty of girl-friends but he never brought them home.

"I'd like you to meet Lily Grace" he announced. He indicated to the tall, slim dark haired young girl at his side. She looked very young.

"Pleased to meet you" said Lily Grace shyly as she went over and kissed Charlotte and Lottie on the cheek and shook Frederick's hand.

"Where is that reprobate brother of mine?" he boomed, "where's young Freddy? I wanted him to be here when I told you my news."

"Oh lord" thought Charlotte, "what's coming now?"

"Freddy is out cavorting no doubt" grumbled Frederick senior, "but he won't get away with it much longer. He'll get called up before long and then he will have to go and do his duty the same as the rest of you.

Neither Frederick or Charlotte were ready for the next words out of Henry's mouth.

"We hope to get married soon" he announced.

"Oh!" exclaimed everyone together. Charlotte still thought she looked very young.

"What do your parents think of that?" she asked.

"My parents are dead" replied Lily. "I was looked after by my brother Joe for a while but now I am in service."

"Oh I am so sorry!" exclaimed Charlotte quite taken aback. She wanted to cut her own tongue out!

"How did you meet?" queried Lottie, coming to the rescue. "Come on, tell all."

Charlotte busied herself in the kitchen getting dinner ready while Frederick carried on polishing his beloved barrel organ.

"Lily works for the Yetts family over at Maybury, met her through Lawrence Yetts who is the son and comes up to the barracks quite frequently. We have had many a drink together."

Frederick, still polishing the barrel organ, thought this was 'true to form'.

In fact Lily was a housemaid for William and Florinda Yetts. William was an Architect and was involved with various projects for the Army. One way and the other their son got to know Henry and they became 'drinking pals' together.

The Gosley family had a very pleasant day with the young couple and, in fact, despite her young age, Charlotte got on very well with Lily Beaven. During the course of the conversation it turned out that she was in fact twenty.

"Ah well" said Charlotte to Frederick after they had left for the train station, "they won't be marrying just yet. She's underage." But she was wrong.

❖ ❖ ❖

Another Christmas passed uneventfully with rationing being the constant worry. It didn't seem right to celebrate when so much carnage was going on elsewhere so it was a subdued affair with only a half hearted attempt to play tunes on the piano and sing carols.

All Lottie wanted was for her Percy to come home safe. She had seen pictures of the devastation on The Somme in the newspapers and the mules carrying masses of equipment. The soldiers, and even the mules were wearing gas masks to protect them against poisonous gases. Would this nightmare never end? All she could think about was Percy. The war had only been going for a few months but already thousands of lives had been lost.

❖ ❖ ❖

1914 gave way to 1915, and the thousands of lives lost were turning into millions, and now the Germans were dropping bombs on London and the East Coast of Britain. The bad news seemed never ending. Then, in the middle of it all Charlotte and Frederick received another bombshell from Henry. It was February and this time he made the trip home on his own. It was obvious the reason for coming home in the foul winter weather had to be for something special. It had taken him best part of the day to come from Woking to Eastbourne by train and his time was very limited. He accepted the enormous bowl of soup from his Mother and then drew a deep breath and gave them his news. Charlotte was ready for anything but not the next words that came out of his mouth.

"Lily Grace and I are getting married at the end of the week."

"What!!?" exclaimed the whole family together.

"The end of the week!" boomed Frederick. "We are at the end of the week – it is Thursday today!"

"Sorry, it was sprung on me a bit because our battalion are being posted overseas – the Russian front I think."

Charlotte could not believe what she was hearing. Had she not felt so proud of him in his uniform she felt like boxing his ears.

"You kept that bloody quiet!" roared Frederick, forgetting for a minute that there were ladies present and little Louise crawling around the floor.

"Well you know what I am like for writing and then I suddenly got told of my posting overseas and everything happened so fast." He paused for breath. "I am so sorry that I didn't tell you beforehand."

The Tailor's Daughter ~ 195

"Well tell us about it now!" Frederick thumped the table with his fist and sent the cups and saucers flying. "It had better be good my lad and where is she anyway?"

"She couldn't get away today as the Yetts family are doing a Charity Dinner, but I thought I would come and tell you personally," he went on manfully. "I don't want to go off to war and just leave her. Who knows when I will be back? At least the Army will provide for her and she will be waiting for me when I return."

Frederick felt like knocking him into the middle of next week for the suddenness of all this, but his anger was tinged with fear and sadness at the idea that his son was off to the Russian front. Charlotte was beginning to admire her son's gallantry. It would not have been right to have left her alone. After all she could be pregnant and it was obvious they were very much in love.

"I thought that it would be best if I came and told you on my own rather than drag her across country for such a short stay, but I have found rooms opposite the barracks and she is to stay there until I come home. There is another army couple living there. It's above the pub!"

"That's my boy" grinned Frederick despite himself. "True to form!"

"Well, it looks as though you have got it all sorted out!" *said Charlotte sarcastically.* She was already feeling more than a little bit miffed at having so little time to prepare.

"*He's bloody cock sure about coming home,*" thought Frederick. There were so many men dying in this war to end all wars – why should his son and son-in-law be any different?

"Well, we will get there on the train" said Charlotte "but I have no time to buy a new hat."

She tried to hide her disappointment. She had missed the wedding of Lottie but at least she had been at the wedding of young Mary to Ernest a few years ago and she had to content herself with that.

As for Freddy, well Charlotte secretly wondered who would have him!

"But she is so young." Pointed out Lottie, "isn't she underage?"

"I darn well hope her brother Joe gave his permission," grunted Frederick.

Henry said nothing and poured his father a port.

As the evening wore on so Charlotte and Frederick learned more about this young girl who they were so soon to be part of their family.

Lily Grace had been one of nine children, no less than five of which had died of the consumption. All five had been girls. The only siblings left were her brothers Joe and Harry and younger sister Mary. Charlotte was horrified.

"Her brother Harry is in the Rifle Brigade and away in the trenches," Henry informed her. "It's all been rotten luck for the girl."

Lottie had been quietly nursing young Louise and at first she had been annoyed with Henry for springing this news on her parents, but she had taken to the girl on her last visit. It seemed such a shame that they would inevitably be living on the other side of the world before long – that is if this horrible war ended and Percy came home safely.

"Come on Lottie" said Charlotte getting up from her chair "let's you and I go and get a bed ready for Henry.

Charlotte's disappointment and Frederick's annoyance subsided throughout the day and overnight, but the following

The Tailor's Daughter ~ 197

morning Henry had to leave. He had to get back to the barracks and Lily for who knows where he would be this time next week.

❖ ❖ ❖

Lily Grace quite liked the flat that Henry had found for her. She would be sharing it with another family and it was less than three miles to Maybury where she could still work for a while for the Yetts family. She really did not know what she would have done without William and Florinda Yetts. She had been barely fourteen when her parents died and she was beside herself with grief. She bad barely got over the death of her sisters. It was her older brother Joe that she and her younger sister Mary and brother Harry turned to for support but the only real answer had been to go into service and Joe knew the Yetts family. Their father. Harry Beaven who was a carpenter at Sandhurst Military Academy, had done work for him. They also had the son Lawrence and a daughter Enid who was the same age as Lily. Although Lily had been the servant she had been treated like one of the family and she would continue to work for them just as long as she could. The head of the family, William Muskett Yetts was an Architect and besides working at Sandhurst he also frequented the Inkerman Barracks where young Henry would be stationed.

Lily looked on as Henry made a few last minute adjustments to his uniform and back pack before proceeding across the road to the barracks and, eventually, the march to the train station and then to who knows where? She was getting to the point of not wanting to hear about this awful war. There was rationing and everyone looked glum and worried. The Germans were dropping bombs from great Zeppelins that could fly over our country at will. Why just recently five of the things killed 71

Londoners right near to where Henry's mother used to live in Clapham and, always, always, always, there were the incessant stories coming back about the carnage in the trenches and men coming home burned and without their limbs.

Lily was beginning to wonder what on earth was going to be in the papers next.

Henry could almost read her mind.

"Don't worry I will be back, I promise you."

She gave him a kiss and watched as he crossed the road to the barracks. It wasn't far but once he had crossed the road and disappeared through the gates she knew it could be ages before she would see him again. It was just as well that nobody knew how long it would actually last.

The war had been on for nearly a year already. Little did she know, as she watched Henry turn and give a final wave that this war had another three years to run and yet the hospitals were already filling up with the injured. In fact, so overrun were they that the big houses that were owned by the gentry were being opened up to care for the wounded.

She turned and went back into the kitchen and felt a wave of sickness come over her. Could it possibly be that she was pregnant?

❖ ❖ ❖

Henry had not been gone more than a month when Lily Grace had a visit from her brother Joe. She knew something was wrong the minute she saw him. He had travelled over from Camberley to see her and he looked very grim faced. With tears welling in his eyes he gave her the news that her beloved brother Harry Beaven had died of wounds received in the trenches on the Somme. She collapsed in a heap in his arms.

The Tailor's Daughter

Her wonderful brother Harry. No, it couldn't be! What else could befall her family?

Thankfully, from Joe's point of view the couple that Lily shared the rooms with were on hand to comfort her so that he could eventually get back home to look after his other sister Mary.

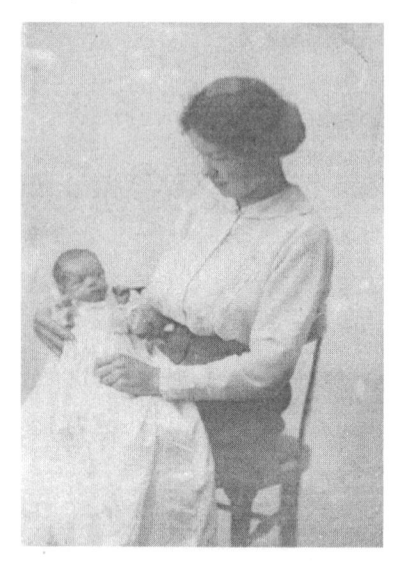

Sarah and John Davies already had a little baby and like Henry, John was in the Army and he too would have to go off to fight. It really was not the news that Sarah wanted to hear, but the two ladies proved to be good comfort and support for each other. Lily found herself wishing that she could go back in time to when she was at school in Camberley and had no worries, but then even that had been fraught with sorrow as first one and then another sister died of TB. At one point her parents even took two of the sisters to Switzerland for the air and their father spent all his savings on the project but it was to no avail. Now she had lost Harry. She felt almost glad that her parents were not around to know about it.

Lily Grace and Lily Dorothy

Henry and Lily's daughter, Lily Dorothy Gosley was born on 22nd September 1915.

❖ ❖ ❖

Charlotte received the news of the birth of a new grandchild with excitement and a keenness to see the baby at the earliest opportunity.

"Oh look Frederick" she squealed waving the letter in the air. "We have a little granddaughter."

"Well let us just hope that Henry is home soon to look after them both." He grunted.

"Oh I shall have to get my knitting needles out again." She laughed. "Life still goes on despite this rotten war."

She watched her husband as he trundled down the road pushing the street organ and wondered how long that would go on for. It didn't seem appropriate somehow to be playing jolly music when there was so much wounding and dying.

Within one month of the news of the new baby young Frederick also joined the Army in the Hampshire Regiment. Now Charlotte was without all her children.

❖ ❖ ❖

(three years later)

On the 11th November 1918 there was a radio broadcast from Paris. "Hostilities will be stopped along the entire front beginning at 11 o'clock on 11th November. The Allied troops will not go beyond the line reached at that hour on that date until further orders."

It was as if the whole world breathed a sigh of relief, not least in the Gosley household.

Percy had already come home just a year ago in 1917 and the little family were still staying with Charlotte and Frederick. It had just seemed like a miracle at the time and for a long while he remained quiet and subdued just shell shocked at the enormity of what he had been through. However he wouldn't talk about it. It was all too painful and he would never get over the loss of all his comrades. However, now a year had passed since his homecoming and he had settled down to a job helping with the fire service until such times as they could go back to Australia or New Zealand.

Charlotte was busy with her sewing when Lottie arrived indoors clutching the newspaper that she had just grabbed from the seller in the street.

"Look everybody" she cried "it's all true, look at the celebrations in London."

Charlotte took the paper and read the content out to Frederick.

> *"London Monday Night. The maroons that in the bad nights of the past beat like blows on the drum of fate gave the news to London at eleven o'clock this morning, and sounded the overture of rejoicing.*
>
> *The idea of using the maroons came right out of the humorous mind of London, and the once terrible sound was like a huge Cockney chuckle of delight. The guns boomed over the heavy grey sky, and everybody knew that the last guns had been fired on the home front."*

"Oh thank God for that" interjected Lottie.

"Quite child," grunted Frederick, "let your Mother continue."

> *"Before the sound had died away innumerable people everywhere rushed into the streets from house, factory and workshop, and children helter-skelter from the schools crying "the war is over!" In a few minutes all over London the little boys in red with the bugles, who used to send us to bed were starting out blowing the cheery 'all clear' for the war. These chubby little angels of goodwill were greeted everywhere with affectionate laughter as they blew away the four years nightmare and all its horrors. The trains on all the lines carried on the note with a wheezy squeal of*

delight. The fat tugs on the river tried to play a tune on one note, and with all these noises mingled the first thin wail of cheers that in a very short time grew loud enough to drown the sound of the maroons. Then the church bells that we have never dared to ring but once on any great day of war, burst into a confident ringing, Big Ben over all, letting themselves go, like all London below them...."

Charlotte continued reading the paper to Frederick and then, as if he just wanted to verify it all he switched his wireless on to listen to the broadcasts about the end of this Great War. Lottie and Percy went off to celebrate leaving their parents to baby-sit.

Within a few days a telegram arrived from Henry to say that he was on his way home. He had a three year old daughter to meet for the first time.

However, it was not good news for everybody. There were so many families in Eastbourne and all over the country who would never see their sons, husbands or fathers again, and many more who will be wounded and scarred for the rest of their lives. One such was William, the boyfriend of her friend Constance. Charlotte paid a visit to Susannah so that she could have company whilst doing her sewing and so that they could help each other. But neither her friend nor her daughters were in a mood for tailoring that morning. They had just received word that William was amongst those that had been brought back home severely wounded.

"He is at some place called Hickwells," said Susannah whilst her daughter dissolved into floods of tears again. We are planning to go and see him. It is at Chailey Green which is over near Lewes."

"I'll come with you," said Charlotte immediately. "It's not too far and we can go by train."

As soon as she had said it she wondered just what she would find there. She knew how terribly wounded some of these soldiers were. However, she had always appreciated the help she received from these women and had grown to class them as true friends. Susannah was well into her sixties now but quite fit and able. Charlotte was just a little bit envious because she had always kept her trim figure as had her daughters. Both the girls were in their early twenties and very pretty. Susannah was widowed and, like Charlotte, had to become her own woman and make her way as best as she could. She once again recalled the words of her father Thomas – "if you can cook or sew you would never grow hungry."

Hickwells was a large rambling country mansion which, like so many, had been given over to the care of the wounded coming back from the front. It stood in its own grounds at the top of Cinder Hill, Chailey Green. The journey by train for the four ladies was uneventful but everywhere there was a mixture of people celebrating the end of the war or others grim faced. It was a combination of the two.

"What lovely grounds" whispered Susannah as they walked through the large gates. "I'll bet there were some gentry lived here once."

Charlotte brought to mind the Brownlow's Mansion where she had been in service all those years ago. They walked through the lawns but soon they realised that the place was overrun with wounded soldiers everywhere. All wore the same serge blue uniform with white lapels. Some were blind, some were on crutches and others had clearly lost limbs. Dotted about among them were the ever caring nurses.

"Oh my God" whispered Margaret, "how awful!"

They walked through the large doors. They were doors that, no doubt, had once been opened for the gentry arriving to a ball or a banquet. Now the place stunk of the wounded. A young nurse, who couldn't have been much older than Constance and Margaret, asked them if she could help them.

"We are looking for William Morris" said Constance tearfully.

The nurse thought for a minute and then, to their relief she remembered where he was.

"Oh yes, William Morris, he is in the Princess Louise Ward." She pointed towards what must have been once a ballroom. The place was packed with wounded soldiers. So crowded was it that hammocks had been slung between the beds so that there was a rest place where normally a nurse could have walked. There were so many men in bandages, some obviously badly burned and some suffering from gas poisoning. Then another nurse came to their aid.

"William Morris?" said Constance hopefully.

"Over there!" said the nurse. They followed her gaze and the young girl immediately recognised him despite the layer of bandages around his face and upper body.

Suddenly he looked up and recognised them and the smile on his face belied the pain he clearly was in.

Constance immediately dissolved into tears.

"There is not enough room for four of us over there" said Susannah, "Constance, why don't you and Margaret go and talk to William and we will wait for you outside."

"Just half an hour" said the nurse kindly. "They all need their rest and there are other visitors to make way for."

Everyone was happy with that. All they wanted to know was that he was all right.

"Come on, lets go out in the gardens," whispered Susannah, "I need some air."

The two of them wandered outside and chatted to one and another of the soldiers who were sitting on benches and taking the air outside. There were hundreds of them and it was a sight that would be mirrored all over the country.

Whilst they were waiting they came across a young woman with two small children. The soldier they were visiting was, like most of the others, wearing the blue uniform with the white lapels.

Charlotte went through her bag and found some sweets.

"Hello" she said to the little girl "what's your name? My name is Charlotte."

"My name is Rosa" she replied "and I am six." She nodded towards the toddler who was clutching the hand of his mother. "This is my brother Stanley, he is four and we are seeing our Daddy."

"Thanks goodness it is all over" said Susannah.

The young woman, who was very beautiful with dark hair tied up in a roll around her head smiled back and nodded in the direction of a group of the soldiers who were all covered in bandages.

"Well at least we have got our men back" she replied. "We have to thank the Lord for that."

Charlotte couldn't help wondering why the Lord had allowed it to happen in the first place but her thoughts were interrupted by the arrival of Constance and Margaret and they took their leave of the little family.

"Thank you for the sweets," said little Stanley as he walked off holding his mother's hand.

Constance looked relieved though tears were still streaming down her face.

"William has been badly burned mother," she said "and he has lost a leg, but he is on the mend and the nurse says she is confident that he will be able to return home within a few months."

The sight of all the men at Chailey Green was something that Charlotte would never forget.

❖ ❖ ❖

15. A New Dawn

(Eight years later – 1929)

Charlotte was really feeling her age now and Frederick was continually ill. She decided that old age was not quite what it was cut out to be and wished she could be back in those heady days of her youth when she went out on the sailing ship to New Zealand. Her husband had long since given up the Street Organ. He persevered with it for a while during the war, but with the continual sight of wounded soldiers, and the worry that everyone was enduring, it somehow seemed out of place. It was a difficult decision because it did provide some light relief amongst the gloom and often people danced in the streets to the tunes he played for them. However, the dancing became less with each horrendous story from the front. In the event, he passed it back to old Harry and it, no doubt, ended up in a museum somewhere.

It was not the weather for strolling along the seafront today though and so Charlotte tucked herself up in her chair and automatically picked up her knitting. She was losing track of how many grandchildren she had now.

Lottie and Percy had a little boy who they called Frank Percy and back in November 1923 they had finally embarked on the SS Suffolk to New Zealand.

Charlotte remembered the day they left so well and how sad she was, but it was their life and she was just grateful that Percy was not one of those millions that had died in the Great War.

She couldn't stand in their way and so for a second time she saw her daughter off to the other side of the world.

It didn't take long for the letters to start flowing back though and the post was quicker now because sometimes they even came by aeroplane. It wasn't long before Charlotte learned that Percy had secured a lease on a Government farm at Hunua near Auckland. It was the other end of the country from Lyttleton Harbour where she had first set foot and met Frederick.

"You should see it Mother" wrote Lottie, "It's one hundred and eight acres and we have a lovely farmhouse. Also," she wrote "I have joined the Women's Institute and am working as their Secretary. and I am starting a dressmaking business just like you did."

Charlotte smiled to herself. She liked the word 'did', as if she didn't do it any more. She still did a bit but had slowed down considerably lately and certainly didn't need all the sewing machines she had. She had given one small one to Lottie, but she still had her father's old treadle that he had used back in Clapham, and her trusty Singer which she still used occasionally. In fact, she had it in mind to make a dress for her oldest granddaughter, Lily Dorothy.

She looked across at Frederick. He really wasn't looking so well lately and she felt that she might have to get the Doctor to him.

Thoughts of Lily Dorothy turned her mind to her son Henry and Lily Grace who were living up in Surrey. Her son had been another of those lucky ones who had come back safely. He had spent most of his war living with a family on the Russian front and sorting out accounts and rations. He had not escaped the bullets completely though and had damage to one eye which would be permanent and shrapnel in his leg.

Again, like most of the men, he did not want to talk about it, not even to his mother and father. It was as if they all had a pact that it would never be spoken about. Within a year of his arrival home Charlotte had another grandchild. A boy this time who they called Harry named after Lily Grace's much loved father and the brother that she had so tragically lost.

There had also been other changes for Henry and Lily which Charlotte was pleased about. He had left the Army but was still working for them at the Inkerman Barracks. He had also secured a house that was altogether bigger for the growing family. It was called Hyde Cottage and down the end of a long lane. Charlotte smiled to herself as she remembered the visit they had paid there soon after Harry was born. They had been determined to see their new grandson and, of course their granddaughter Lily Dorothy, Frederick also wanted to see where his son was living and so they arranged for Wilfred to take them by car. It had been quite an adventure in itself across the country and stopping every so often to fill up with petrol or visit some hostelry. He had changed his old car for a newer one and at least it boasted a roof now, so you didn't have to sit up high with a cover over your hat to stop it blowing off, but it was still a long journey and Charlotte thought her backside would never be the same again.

"Do you remember when we went to Henry's house?" giggled Charlotte.

"|I certainly do" laughed Frederick "I thought my bones were going to fall out going down that bumpy lane."

"Poor Wilfred, he thought his new car would fall apart like one at a circus – it was so precious to him!"

It had indeed been a very bumpy lane, but it was a nice enough house with an outside privy. Charlotte wished that they had a flush privy like she had but not everyone had one yet, not by any means. Even now in 1929 there were still plenty of people with tin buckets that had to be emptied almost every day. There were two houses side by side but they were in the end one nearest to the lane with a nice little garden in the front and plenty of space at the back for the children to play. But the main thing was that Henry had got home in one piece and Lily Grace could try and put the sadness at the loss of her brother behind her. Henry working in the Pay Office for the Army hadn't quite been what Frederick had envisaged for him. He had trained to be a teacher, but he seemed to be doing well and providing for his children and that was all that mattered.

"Where have the years gone Frederick?" Charlotte said out loud. "Where have the years gone?"

She put down her knitting and went across and closed the curtains. It was only five o'clock and yet already it was getting dark. She thought again about Lottie all those miles away on the other side of the world. It would be just getting light there now and the children would be waking up to face the day. It seemed like a lifetime ago that she had first set foot on New Zealand soil herself after that hazardous journey across the oceans. She pulled herself up short – "it was a lifetime ago you silly woman!" she said to no-one in particular.

Now you could get to New Zealand in six weeks or so and in considerably more comfort than she had experienced and some people could even go by aeroplane.

She picked up a photograph that Lily Grace had just sent her and her mind turned back to Henry and her daughter-in-law. It had been taken just outside the cottage that she had visited with Frederick and Wilfred. The family had certainly increased since Lily Dorothy was born. Besides young Harry, there was

Frederick, then little Phyllis and finally baby Frank. Lily Grace was also pregnant again.

"I think I may have a bit more knitting to do," she thought. She smiled to herself ironically. There were some benefits to getting married late in life – or were there? Lily Grace was so young and she had five children already. Charlotte had not even met Frederick at the age Lily was and so could keep her family to a reasonable size. By the time she'd had five children she was too old to have any more, but Lily had time.

"Oh I wonder what the future holds for them?" mused Charlotte.

She laughed at the thought of her own father who could not cope with the 'contraptions' on the roads, and further back still to old Jonathan Adshead, her Grandfather who had been born into a London in the seventeen hundreds and knew nothing else but horses on the streets.

"I wonder what he would make of it all?" she said out loud.

"Who?" said Frederick.

"My old Granddad Jonathan," she laughed, "old rogue that he was. Married four times you know."

"Once is enough my dear!" muttered Frederick, "once is enough."

She ignored his little joke and wondered again what old Jonathan or even her father would think of life today. Now cars clogged the roads and aeroplanes could fly across the channel and even, with stops along the way, to Australia and New Zealand. It had been eleven years since the Great War and now times were not bad, especially for young people. Since the war the whole atmosphere in Britain had changed. Women's fashions had changed and she noticed that the young people were wearing shorter skirts and showing much more stocking. Not that she ever would. She would stick to the long dress she had always worn!

People generally were still celebrating that it was all over without ever forgetting the sacrifices made. She had even been to the Cinema to see Charlie Chaplin along with her daughter Mary and she had laughed so much she thought she would split her sides. Yes things were changing very fast and people were making the most of it. After all, it had been the 'War to end all wars', hadn't it?

"I wonder if it really was the war to end all wars?" she said as she picked up the paper ready to read its contents to Frederick.

"I wonder!" said Frederick.

She studied the photo again and reminded herself that she must go to the shops and buy a frame for it. Her heart went out to fourteen year old Lily Dorothy who was just about to go out into service the day after the photograph was taken.

"Oh dear," she said, "Lily Dorothy doesn't look very happy at all does she Frederick?"

"Did you the day before you were sent off into service?" he replied.

She laughed.

"No I don't suppose I did. Cleaning somebody else's house was the last thing I wanted to do and I still think it is unfair that girls should have to do this and that the boys get taught a trade."

"Oh not that old moan again!" he cried. "Charlotte, it will never happen darling!"

"Oh yes it will" she replied. "Oh yes it will." She was still gloating because women had only just got the vote last year. Frederick had been horrified.

She could sense that Frederick was becoming agitated and decided that she had better be tactful. She put down the photo

The Tailor's Daughter ~ 213

of Lily Grace and her growing family and went to make him some tea, but she was feeling rather smug about women getting the vote after all this time.

❖ ❖ ❖

In fact Charlotte had been right. Lily Dorothy was not feeling very happy at all. They had been entertaining her Auntie Mary from Camberley, her mother's sister and she had been landed with all the washing up.

"It will give you good practice," Henry said a little unsympathetically. There was a lot of washing up for eight in the old stone sink and she had to fetch the water from the well. Her father had been very taken with his new camera and was anxious to take a picture of them all – "for posterity" he said.

Lily knew what a camera was. In fact they were quite common but Henry had never owned one until now.

She put down the soap and dried her hands while Henry tried to gather all his family together for the photograph. She did not like being reminded that she was off to be a Scullery Maid, and like her grandmother before her she wondered why it was always the boys that had the extra education and the apprenticeships.

"Come on, hurry up Lily," cried young Harry, "while it is still light outside, stop being a slowcoach."

She felt like throwing the tea towel at him but she quickly followed the family outside with her sleeves still rolled up to her elbows and wondering how she was going to cope with washing up all day and every day as a Scullery Maid. She was closely followed by her Aunt and the tall slim figure of her mother. It was quite a performance to get the little ones to stand in front.

Little Phyllis and baby Frank thought it all very funny whilst the two older boys were just embarrassed.

"Stand still!" roared Henry, "the picture will be all fuzzy if you move. I want to send it to your Grandparents at Eastbourne."

Lily Grace with her youngest sister Mary. In the centre, Lily Dorothy, Frederick, Harry, and in the foreground little Phyllis and baby Frank.

Henry remembered back to when his mother wanted to have their picture taken when he was a child and he had to stand stock still and 'watch the birdie'. What a performance that had been. Cameras had moved on a bit since then and he was very proud of the box Brownie he had recently acquired.

Lily didn't see her Grandparents at Eastbourne very often but she knew everything about them as her Father was always telling the children about Frederick and all his ancestors who earned their living from the sea. He even had a picture on his wall of a seafaring man sitting on a rock pointing out across the ocean. It was his pride and joy and reminded him of where he was brought up in Sussex. He had a record that you could put on a machine called a gramophone and it played 'Sussex by the Sea'.

She had been taken on the train to Eastbourne when she was younger but since the family had grown they rarely went very far. Now her whole life was going to change. She wondered what life would have in store for her being in service. Would she, one day, meet a handsome young man who would sweep her off her feet? Would she travel like her Grandma Charlotte? She really hoped she would not have a lot of children who would die as her Grandma Beaven had. She had so many thoughts rushing around in her head as she stood and patiently waited for her father to take his picture.

Henry, satisfied that he had got the image he wanted, allowed the younger ones to go off and play whilst Lily went back to the washing up and the boys to their studies. His views on female equality remained the same as his father's!

Auntie Mary started her long walk home across the fields to Camberley and he gallantly escorted her for part of the way.

Lily Dorothy wished she were going to Camberley too. She was quite used to going across the fields and taking the younger children with her. It was a long walk but worth it because she could see her Uncle Joe, her mother's older brother who was really like a Granddad to her, but she knew those days were going to be over and a new phase in her life was just beginning.

Just like her mother and her grandmother before her, and probably her great grandmother before that, she was off out into the service of the gentry.

❖ ❖ ❖

Charlotte put the photo down. She knew just how young Lily Dorothy must be feeling. She did hope that one day she would be fortunate and meet someone nice. The years had gone so quickly and it seemed hardly credible that it was already nearly fifty years since she had first set foot on New Zealand soil and caught sight of the handsome Frederick Gosley at the 'Sailors Return'. He had been able to see in those days.

Frederick finished his tea, pulled himself up out of his chair and went over and gave her a kiss. No, he did not look well.

"I think I will go to bed now dear," he said, "I'm not feeling so good – perhaps a good night's sleep will be the thing."

She watched him as he shuffled out of the room. He looked so much like his father James Morehouse Gosley now, and once again she marvelled at how fast the years had slipped away. She had few regrets though other than the loss of baby James who had been given her father-in-laws name. She had made her own adventures and had the courage to go all that way to New Zealand all by herself. Now, from the point of view of a woman in her seventies she marvelled at her own rashness. *"I must have been mad"* she thought to herself, and then giggled out loud. Then she remembered how ill Frederick had looked as he made his way to the stairs and made a decision that the following day she would get him to go and see the doctor.

Frederick Timothy Gosley died in March 1929. He was 78.

❖ ❖ ❖

The Tailor's Daughter ~ 217

Charlotte was devastated at the death of Frederick. He was well known in Eastbourne and the funeral was attended by all the family including Henry and Lily and many of their friends. Young Lily Dorothy had to take the day off working for the gentry in order to look after the younger children while they were away.

The new widow had coped while there were things to do and visitors to look after, but even they had to go at some time and now, as she settled back into an empty house she had to reflect on a life alone.

But she was not a woman to give up. She had even more time to do her dressmaking and her knitting but life would certainly never be the same for her again. She closed her eyes and thought of that young girl, Charlotte Adshead, who had suddenly upped and left her home in Clapham and all the things that had happened since, both within the family and within the wider world. She had gone from horses on the streets of London to aeroplanes in the air.

One major thing, in Charlotte's eyes, to happen was the granting of Votes for Women. Despite her desolation at her loss she laughed out loud as she thought of Frederick's face when she read the news to him. He had been horrified – bless him. She could hear him now – "it will never happen Charlotte, it will never happen."

To his grave he had been a 'male chauvinist,' but she loved him for all that and her life was all but over.

Her daughter Mary paid her a visit along with her husband Ernest, still wearing black and mourning the loss of her father, and even young Freddy was less boisterous as he recalled his father and how manfully he had tackled his blindness. Everyone still called him 'young' Frederick, even though he was now well into his thirties and had seen active service in the Hampshire Regiment.

Mary caught sight of the photograph that Lily Grace had sent. It was propped on the mantelpiece still waiting for Charlotte to put it in a frame. Just something she had been meaning to do but had not got around to.

"That's a nice one of them all mother!" she exclaimed as she peered at it closely. "My, aren't they all growing up now?"

She picked it up and studied it through a haze of tears.

"Who is the lady standing behind my niece Lily Dorothy? I've not seen her before."

"I think that is Lily's sister," she replied, "Henry's sister-in-law."

Mary studied the photo again. She, of course knew the children but she did not see them very often,

"I wonder what the future holds for them all?" she said. "There have been so many changes since the Great War."

"Please God they never see another War such as that," said Charlotte. Let us hope that it really was the 'War to end all Wars'. I don't think I shall ever forget seeing those poor men at Chailey Green."

"Just imagine daughter," she said, changing the subject, "When I was your age there were no cars on the road and look at it now."

".....and," smiled Mary, sensing a way to get a smile back to her mother's face, "and you did not have Votes for Women."

The two women burst into laughter despite the sadness of the occasion.

Charlotte went over to the dresser and helped herself to some of Frederick's best Port and poured out two small glassfuls.

"Come on Mary." She smiled "let's drink to Emily Pankhurst."

The Tailor's Daughter ~ 219

"Also to father," said Mary. "Also to father."
They raised their glasses together.

Never really recovering from the death of Frederick, Charlotte died just nine months after him in December 1929. She was 71.

❖ ❖ ❖

In fact, despite everyone hoping that the Great War was the 'war to end all wars'. Lily Dorothy would see another one in just ten years time and it would be equally as devastating. However, she would also, one day, be able to look at a box in the corner of the room with moving pictures on it showing men standing on the moon. Where it took Charlotte three months to get to New Zealand her granddaughter would know of people who could do it in an aeroplane and take little more than a day. Both Lily's young brother Harry and little Phyllis would end up living in Canada and making lives for themselves there. As for young Fred – well he followed in the footsteps of his Auntie Charlotte (or Lottie) and his Grandmother and he took his young family to New Zealand.

Charlotte's father Thomas Adshead had thought the motor car was an abomination that pushed the horses off the streets but the children in the photograph that Henry had taken would know of aeroplanes going faster than sound and roads clogged with nothing else but cars and they too would wonder what it would be like for the generation that would come after them.

As for Votes for Women, Lily Dorothy would see a woman on the Throne of England and a woman Prime Minister – stuff that would make her ancestors choke on their dinners. But, more than that, her days of being a Scullery Maid would end and she would meet a handsome young man just as Grandma Charlotte hoped she would.

She would also inherit the precious Singer sewing machine that had belonged to the Tailors Daughter which she would use to make clothes for her own children.

How do I know all this? Because Lily Dorothy was my mother and the handsome young man she married in 1939 was my father and the two of them really did live happily ever after.

As for the handsome young man well, in 1915 when he was four years old, he visited Chailey Green with his mother and his sister Rosa and a nice lady called Charlotte gave him some sweets.

~ End ~

About the Author

Joan Blackburn was born in Woking in 1941. Her first book 'Naafi, Knickers & Nijmegen' was published in 2009 and told of her adventures in the WRAF between 1959 and 1963. With the success of this tale of Air Force life in the swinging sixties Joan was encouraged to go back a generation for her second book 'Granddad's Rainbow'. This told of life on the home front both during and immediately after the war and featured her parents, Lily and Stan. It is against the, fast disappearing, upstairs/downstairs life of her grandparents where they worked for the gentry and also against the background of Stan's life in the RAF serving in France and Malta and the steadfastness of Lily as she waited for him to come home.

Now, with 'The Tailor's Daughter' Joan has gone back still further to the Victorian life of her Great Grandmother on Lily's side of the family, who, in the 1880s set sail for New Zealand on her own. Lily's maiden name was Gosley. Her grandfather married the plucky Charlotte Adshead and the decision they were forced to make, soon after their marriage, affected every generation thereafter. This trilogy of books cover 150 years of family history.

Joan is married to Norman Blackburn and lives in West Sussex. She has two children, Catherine and David, and four small grandchildren, Jacob, Alice, Harvey and Keira. This book is about their Great Great Great Grandmother.